"Partners in Progress"
by Sheila Walsh Guenther and Busse Nutley

Foreword by Milton Bona

Produced in Cooperation with
the Greater Vancouver Chamber of Commerce

Windsor Publications, Inc.
Northridge, California

VANCOUVER on the Columbia

An Illustrated History

Ted Van Arsdol

This book is dedicated to Dr. John Brougher, a fine gentleman, a physician who delivered many hundreds of Clark County babies, and a history enthusiast who inspired others with his attitude on preserving the artifacts and records of the past. He was a frequent president of Fort Vancouver Historical Society.

Windsor Publications, Inc.—History Book Division

Publisher: John M. Phillips
Editorial Director: Teri Davis Greenberg
Design Director: Alexander D'Anca

Staff for *Vancouver on the Columbia*
Editor: Jerry Mosher
Assistant Editors: Laura Cordova, Marilyn Horn
Editorial Development: Teri Davis Greenberg
Director, Corporate Biographies: Karen Story
Assistant Director, Corporate Biographies: Phyllis Gray
Editor, Corporate Biographies: Judith Hunter
Production Director, Corporate Biographies: Una
    FitzSimons
Layout Artist, Corporate Biographies: Mari Catherine
    Preimesberger
Sales Representatives, Corporate Biographies: David
    Cook, Elizabeth Cook
Editorial Assistants: Kathy M. Brown, Marcie Goldstein,
    Pamela Juneman, Pat Pittman
Proofreader: Susan J. Muhler
Designer: J.R. Vasquez
Layout Artist: Cheryl Carrington

Library of Congress Cataloging in Publication Data
Van Arsdol, Ted.
    Vancouver on the Columbia.

    "Produced in cooperation with the Greater Vancouver
Chamber of Commerce."
    Bibliography: p. 154
    Includes index.
    1. Vancouver (Wash.)—History. 2. Vancouver
(Wash.)—Description. 3. Vancouver (Wash.)—Industries.
I. Greater Vancouver Chamber of Commerce (Wash.)
II. Title.
F899.V2V34   1986   979.7'86   86-24549
ISBN 0-89781-102-X

Frontispiece: *The future of the spectacular Columbia Gorge is a topic of debate between environmental groups and individuals wanting to develop homesites and other projects. The gorge starts at the east end of Clark County and extends eastward through the Cascade Mountains for many miles.*

Contents

Acknowledgments

Vancouver on the Columbia has benefited from the aid and active interest of many people.

Staff members at Windsor Publications offered helpful guidelines and other assistance. Especially notable were Teri Davis Greenberg, the first editor of the manuscript, and Jerry Mosher, who edited the work in its final months of preparation.

Milt Bona of Camas provided invaluable assistance by reading the manuscript for accuracy. Victoria Ransom, secretary of the Fort Vancouver Historical Society, also read part of the manuscript, and her help is appreciated. The author, however, takes responsibility for any errors.

My wife, Carole, patiently spent many hours typing the chapters, captions, and other information needed by the publishers.

The Vancouver *Columbian,* where the author formerly was employed, gave substantial support by loaning pictures from its extensive files. Susan Seyl and her co-workers in the photo archives at the Oregon Historical Society at Portland provided many other pictures, and Hermine Decker copied photos from Clark County Museum.

The major facilities used in researching Vancouver history were the Oregon Historical Society's library, the Vancouver Community Library, and the Clark County Museum operated by the Fort Vancouver Historical Society and the Heritage Trust of Clark County.

Ted Van Arsdol
Vancouver, Washington
June 1986

Hardy boaters will venture onto the Columbia River in almost any kind of weather, but the advent of warm, sunny days brings the greatest turnout of all types of pleasure boats. Mount Hood provides a backdrop as a young man watches boats from the riverside.

Foreword

Hudson's Bay Company officials first turned their attention to the Columbia River in 1821 when they merged with their bitter rival, the British-owned North West Company. The merger included the former American trading post, Astoria, which the North West Company had purchased a few years before. Sir George Simpson, Hudson's Bay's western governor, chose Dr. John McLoughlin, lately with North West, to head the company's new Columbia River department. His assignment was to trap beaver and trade as many pelts as he could.

After surveying the situation at Astoria, Simpson and McLoughlin decided to relocate the company's headquarters inland, choosing the present site of Vancouver. Here a stockade and living quarters were built, and in 1825 Simpson christened the establishment Fort Vancouver in honor of Captain George Vancouver, who had discovered and explored much of the Pacific Northwest a generation earlier.

For twenty-one years the Oregon country, which originally included western British Columbia, was the exclusive domain of the Hudson's Bay Company. From Vancouver McLoughlin ruled an area more than three times the size of the United Kingdom; a benevolent despot, he represented both king and company.

As word of the rich Oregon country reached the new United States, a few hardy Americans braved the elements and the Indians to come and settle. McLoughlin sold them food and supplies, often on credit, knowing that otherwise they would starve. He directed all newcomers to the lush and fertile Willamette Valley south of the Columbia River, because his company and the British government had hopes of establishing the Columbia as the southern boundary of Canada.

The American migration developed from a trickle to a torrent, and by 1844 many Americans were settling north of the Columbia in the Puget Sound area as well. By the time American and British authorities met in 1846 to settle the boundary dispute between the United States and Canada, the Oregon country had all the sights and sounds of an American colony. Their treaty set the border 300 miles north of the Columbia River at the 49th parallel; the reign of the British Hudson's Bay Company would soon come to an end.

Three years later American soldiers arrived at Vancouver and established a military post. Without firing a shot the young United States had acquired one of the greatest territorial prizes of all time.

Milton Bona, Editor Emeritus
Fort Vancouver Historical Society

October 25, 1958—The new Clark College buildings and campus were dedicated.

February 15, 1961—The City Council approved an urban renewal project covering fifty-five acres, a total of twenty-eight blocks.

October 12, 1962—Clark County was hit by a windstorm that caused a great amount of property damage.

March 2, 1965—After considerable negotiation and controversy, Gilmore Steel announced it had dropped plans for a plant at Vancouver.

July 27, 1966—A local group began plans to raise money to build a new hospital after the Sisters of Charity of Providence decided to quit operating St. Joseph Hospital.

October 17, 1967—St. Joseph Community Hospital, Inc., took over from the sisters and began leasing the hospital. A fund drive had been started for a new building.

August 25, 1970—Residents learned that a Sky River rock festival was being planned near Washougal. The event in late August and early September drew thousands of youths from many states and was a major Clark County topic for several weeks.

February 27, 1972—St. Joseph Community Hospital started welcoming visitors at a one-week open

---

The House of Providence, designed by Mother Joseph and opened in 1873, served as headquarters for the Sisters of Charity of Providence. The structure also housed a girls' school, Providence Academy. In recent years the building has been owned by the Hidden family, and businesses and offices have occupied its restored interior. Photo by Ed Vidinghoff

house. Patients were moved from the old hospital a month later.

April 5, 1972—A tornado destroyed Peter Ogden Elementary School and caused considerable other damage.

March 2, 1973—After several years of controversy, the Port of Portland abandoned its plan to expand runways into the Columbia River by dredging, though expansion was scheduled to move ahead on the mainland. Some of the most vociferous objections to the river plan had come from Vancouver.

January 13, 1975—The Vancouver City Council approved an ordinance authorizing card rooms. This was a follow-up to a vote of residents in November 1974 favoring such a plan. In 1982 the council began discussion of phasing out the controversial card rooms, and in 1983 set a deadline to eliminate the businesses by the end of 1984.

June 19, 1975—Soviet pilots Georgi Baidukov and Alexander Belyakov arrived at Pearson Airpark for the dedication of a monument commemorating their transpolar flight of 1937.

August 12, 1975—The boards of Vancouver's two hospitals approved a management consolidation plan for the facilities. On September 23, 1977, the Washington State Department of Social and Health Services gave final approval to a merger of the two hospitals.

December 20, 1976—The City Council decided to contract with the Portland-area Tri-Met bus agency to take over Vancouver-Portland bus service after a local operator announced plans to quit business on December 31.

1977—City and county workers went on strike. The eight-day strike of 270 county workers ended February 4. One hundred and seventy Vancouver city workers struck from January 20 to February 7.

March 13, 1980—Trustees of St. Joseph and Vancouver Memorial hospitals decided to rescind an action to close Vancouver Memorial. The closure had been announced in late 1979 and had led to protests from many residents. Under a revised plan, each hospital was to have its own specialties.

May 18, 1980—Mount St. Helens erupted, blowing off its top and devastating a large area. This area sensation also was the biggest story of the year for Washington State.

The Interstate bridges connecting Vancouver and Portland have increased in importance with the area's population growth. Congestion on the spans was eased when the bridge carrying Interstate Highway 205 was completed in 1982, but traffic volume on the older bridges has been rising again in recent years.

July 7, 1981—After years of discussion, the City Council voted that Cox Cable should get a franchise for cable television service. On the following day, Clark County commissioners also approved the Cox proposal.

August 28-29, 1981—The Columbia Arts Center, the city's first performing arts center, celebrated its opening with a street festival and other activities.

October 22, 1982—A gate was opened, allowing water from the Columbia River to flow in and flush polluted water out of Vancouver Lake. This was considered a benchmark in the Port of Vancouver's long-range efforts to rehabilitate the shallow lake, a plan first announced in 1968.

December 15, 1982—The Interstate Highway 205 Bridge was opened, connecting Vancouver with east Portland.

September 4, 1984—The U.S. General Services Administration presented a deed for Officers' Row to the City of Vancouver. City officials later planned to develop the former section of historic Vancouver Barracks for an executive conference center, offices, residences, and shops.

December 31, 1984—Gamblers quit play at downtown cardrooms. Cardroom operators had lost a ballot item in the November election that would have overturned a City Council decision to end the games on December 31. Voters rejected the cardrooms again in an 1985 election.

April 9, 1985—Ground was broken for Kyocera Corporation's $30 million manufacturing and ceramic research center. The first phase of the plant began operations in December.

August 22, 1985—General Brewing Company announced that brewing at its Vancouver plant would cease the following day, and packaging would stop when inventories were depleted. Much of its equipment was eventually shipped to China. The brewery dated from the 1850s.

May 5, 1986—James River Corp. of Richmond, Virginia, officially took control of the Crown Zellerbach paper plant at Camas. The subsidiary retained its old name.

June 2, 1986—Three potlines of the Aluminum Company of America smelter shut down when employees joined a nationwide strike against Alcoa plants. Two days later, Alcoa reported that it was closing the Vancouver smelter permanently, affecting about 500 jobs. The facility had been plagued for a long time by financial troubles.

June 6, 1986—Port of Vancouver commissioners signed a four-year lease with Matsushita Kotobuki Electronics Industries Inc. The company, based in Osaka, Japan, planned to assemble color TV sets and manufacture videocassette recorders in port warehouses for General Electric Co. Investment in equipment for the Matsushita facilities was expected to reach $20 million.

In 1847 Paul Kane painted these Chinook Indians outside their lodge near Vancouver. Mild temperatures eliminated the need for much clothing among natives of the lower Columbia, and the annual migratory runs of salmon and steelhead provided them with a food bonanza. The natives' diet was supplemented by berries and nutritious wapato root. Courtesy, Royal Ontario Museum, Toronto, Canada

The Natives and the Fort

Despite a strong difference of opinion about who should occupy the part of the Oregon Territory north of the Columbia River, Massachusetts schoolteacher Hall J. Kelley and the Hudson's Bay Company were in agreement about at least one thing. Both considered Vancouver a fine site for a new settlement.

Kelley, who was called the "Prophet of Oregon," visited the Vancouver area in 1834. He was an enthusiastic promoter for U.S. expansion into the Pacific Northwest, including the region north of the Columbia River:

The prospect is one of the loveliest on which my eye ever rested, diversified by all that is wild, rugged and sublime, in forest and mountain scenery, or soft and smiling in lowland and meadow, river and plain.

In the distance . . . are the snowy peaks . . . Nearer at hand is a vast ocean of forest, variegated with every hue known to the foliage of trees . . . At your feet are a thousand appearances of industry, wealth and prosperity.

Kelley's interests conflicted with those of Hudson's Bay Company officials such as George Simpson, who, like Kelley, admired the Vancouver area. Simpson said he had "rarely seen a Gentleman's Seat [estate] in England possessing so many natural advantages and where ornament and use are so agreeably combined."

The Hudson's Bay Company had established Fort Vancouver in 1825 on a plain overlooking the Columbia near a great forest, with a beautiful view of snowcapped Mount Hood fifty miles to the southeast. From Vancouver the company developed a considerable trade with California, the Hawaiian Islands, and Russian Alaska.

Not long after the establishment of the fort, Dr. John McLoughlin, the fort's chief factor, took note of the surrounding environment that provided salmon, steelhead, and wapato root (arrowhead) for the Indians. In an 1826-1827 report he remarked that although a considerable number of beaver remained in the region, the Indians did not feel much incentive to trap them for the British. They did not need the provisions, and temperatures were so mild they

CHAPTER

I

Above: *A cart of the Red River variety stands in the fore-ground of this peaceful scene depicting Fort Vancouver circa 1845. The artist is unknown. Kanaka Village, occupied by fort employees and their families, was located just outside the Hudson's Bay Company stockade. Courtesy, Fort Vancouver National Historic Site*

Opposite page, top: *The British flag still flew over Fort Vancouver in 1845 when Lieutenant Henry Warre visited, but the increasing population of Americans in the Willamette Valley made the Hudson's Bay Company control seem tenuous. Warre painted this scene complete with strolling Indians and frontiersmen. Courtesy, Fort Vancouver National Historic Site*

Opposite page, bottom: *Fluvia Kerr painted this replica of a giant Hudson's Bay Company flag which was said to have flown over Fort Vancouver starting with its dedication in 1825. The Latin legend "Pro Pelle Cutem" is said to mean "You give your skin to get a skin," referring to the hazards of the fur trade. Photo by Ed Vidinghoff*

Ships of competing maritime nations explored the Northwest coast and opened a trading era with the tribes. This painting by F.P. Thursby portrays natives greeting Captain George Vancouver's Discovery, *and the* Chatham. *The ships visited the area near the mouth of the Columbia. Courtesy, Clark County Museum*

did not even need many clothes from the fur company's stores. "The only covering they use is a rat skin blanket," McLoughlin wrote. "The woolens they buy from us are merely to please their fancy."

The inhabitants of Fort Vancouver were not the first to encounter these Northwest Indians. Lieutenant William Broughton had found the natives flourishing when he staked a British claim to the country in 1792, not long after U.S. Captain

Robert Gray had discovered the mouth of the river and named it for his vessel, the *Columbia Rediviva.* Broughton took the armed tender *Chatham* up the Columbia to a point near present-day Washougal, accompanied by numerous canoes of Indians on the river adjacent to what is now Clark County. Broughton had been sent out by Captain George Vancouver of the ship *Discovery,* which did not enter the mouth of the river.

In 1805-1806 the Lewis and Clark Expedition found numerous Indian villages along the same stretch of the Columbia River, and definite signs of white traders who had come by sea. The natives, adept in canoes, had access to the lower river where goods from the traders' ships were available. One group of Indians encountered by the U.S. Army party in November 1805 in the Vancouver area was garbed in scarlet and blue blankets, sailor jackets, overalls, shirts, and hats, in addition to their usual native costume. Corruption from some of these early meetings with whites was evident in the words of an Indian in a passing canoe: he used the word "blackguard" and other English curse words.

The Indians of the Vancouver area and other parts of the lower river were skilled craftsmen. Patrick Gass and Sergeant John Ordway of the Lewis and Clark Expedition praised the excellent quality of their canoes. A little later, Gilbert Franchere, working out of Astoria, was impressed by the natives' patience in getting cedar for the construction of homes, which were sometimes very spacious, as much as 100 feet long.

The Indians living along the Columbia were called Chinooks, though several other names were used by Lewis and Clark in the first detailed account of the tribes. They all spoke a common trade language called Chinookan. One group, called the Shoto, numbered 460 and resided in eight houses at Vancouver Lake, described in the party's journals as a pond. Near this encampment was Lake River, an easy connection to the Columbia.

The first major U.S. effort to establish trade with natives of the interior was made by John Jacob Astor's Pacific Fur Company, organized in 1810. In the following year it built Fort Astoria at the mouth of the Columbia, and after some initial difficulties the company began to make progress in trading. But the War of 1812 intervened. No supply ship was sent to Astoria that year, and the British Navy planned to take the fort. Before British ships arrived, however, an overland party of the North West Company came to the area and raised a British flag. Anticipating the arrival of British warships, a Pacific Fur Company official in charge of the fort sold the property to the North West Company, which renamed it Fort George. Astor later said that the price was well below its real value, but the sale did keep British sailors from plundering the fort when they finally arrived.

In 1821 the North West Company merged with the Hudson's Bay Company. Four years later the company's headquarters for the Columbia River was moved from Fort George to what is now Vancou-

While trading for sea otters in 1792, American Captain Robert Gray, the commander of the Columbia Rediviva, *discovered the mouth of the Columbia River. Gray named the river after his ship. Courtesy, Oregon Historical Society (neg. no. 132)*

ver. Here the company could grow crops and raise cattle on a large scale. The first Fort Vancouver was constructed at the site of the present Washington State School for the Deaf on Grand Boulevard, about one mile east of the later fort. Simpson, Hudson's Bay governor for the region, dedicated the fort on March 19, 1825, by breaking a bottle of rum on the fort flagstaff.

From the fort's earliest days, the dispatching of parties to trap and trade was an important part of the company's activity. Especially hazardous expeditions journeyed to the Snake River area under the leadership of Peter Skene Ogden in the late 1820s.

Above: *Sir George Simpson, who served as governor for the Hudson's Bay Company over an extensive part of North America, dedicated Fort Vancouver in 1825. He visited the Columbia several times, and kept close account of fur trading at the fort. Courtesy, Oregon Historical Society (neg. no. 54480)*

Ogden commented in 1827 of such duties: "This life makes a young man sixty in a few years."

One of the first prominent Americans to arrive at the fort was fur trader Jedediah Smith, who sought adventure. He and four others were the only survivors of a party attacked by Indians in late 1828 on the Umpqua River. The Hudson's Bay Company had sent out the party to retrieve loot taken by the Indians from the Americans. Smith stayed until March 1829 at Fort Vancouver, which he described as situated on "a handsome prairie."

Indians also began to visit the fort. One of the most notable sights there in the late 1820s must have been the arrival of an Indian chief. The dignitary came from the mouth of the Columbia, preceded by 300 slaves. The slaves carpeted the chief's walkway from the fort entrance to McLoughlin's door with beaver and otter skins. The Reverend

Pierre-Jean De Smet, who mentioned the chief's style of entry, visited his grave a few years later near Astoria. The chief had died during an epidemic that killed much of the native population on the lower river.

A sawmill, the first in the Northwest, was built several miles upriver from the fort around 1828. Shipbuilding also was started in the 1820s. Later, ships were purchased or built in England for the Hudson's Bay trade.

In 1829 Fort Vancouver was moved to its final site, a short distance east of what is now Interstate Highway 5. The old location had been abandoned because of lack of water and its distance from the river.

George T. Allan, who came to the fort as an employee in 1831, left a description of one of the most colorful fort scenes—the comings and goings of expeditions. Brigades from Vancouver penetrated

Below: *Peter Skene Ogden, a former member of the North West Company, joined the Hudson's Bay organization and was appointed a chief factor in 1835. Courtesy, Oregon Historical Society (neg. no. 707)*

Even when the main gate at Fort Vancouver was closed, people could enter or depart through a small door like the one shown here. This north wall was rebuilt about 1973. Courtesy, National Park Service

as far southeast as Utah, and frequently traveled into Oregon and even into the Sacramento Valley. Allan wrote:

The months of June and July were generally a busy time at Vancouver, when from the 1st to the 10th of June, at which season the Columbia is high, the Brigade of Boats, as they were called, descended from the interior with the furs and carried back the winter supplies.

Then the men composing the crews, principally Canadians, Iroquois and half-breeds, would be indulged, after their long abstinence, with an allowance of liquor, pork and flour, as a regale; then would come the tug of war, with many bloody noses and black eyes, but never with any fatal result.

After the departure of the boats, The Snake party of trappers would arrive, headed by Mr. [John] Work, who had then succeeded Mr. Ogden . . . as head of trappers into the Snake and Blackfeet countries, often a perilous undertaking, as during my time at Vancouver these parties have returned

with wounded men, and left several killed behind them.

The mode adopted with the trappers was to furnish their supplies at a moderate rate, and allow them a fair price for their furs . . . The horses and traps were also furnished them, and on being returned, placed to their credit.

In the Bachelors Hall at the fort, returning travelers met frequently for a convivial evening of talk and tale-spinning. Among these tale-tellers was McLoughlin's stepson, the half-Indian Thomas McKay. Allan remembered McKay smoking a long-stemmed clay pipe filled with tobacco and an intoxicating weed used by the Indians, telling "long sulphurous stories," some fanciful. McKay thrived on the most desperate situations the company could find for him. He was a terror to the Indians and was considered by Governor Simpson to be a human "bloodhound," a necessary evil at a place such as Vancouver, according to Simpson.

Despite shows of friendship, conflicts with Indians did occur, usually in more remote areas such as the Snake River area. Nearer the fort Indians became less of a factor in the early 1830s because of an epidemic. Fever and ague first broke out along the Columbia in 1829; Indians believed a ship anchored nearby had brought the malady. The epidemic during the next two years decimated entire villages, and on September 25, 1830, McLoughlin wrote that "the intermittent fever is making a dreadful havoc among the natives and at this place half our people are laid up with it." In an October 11 letter he estimated that three-fourths of the Indians in the fort's vicinity had been "carried off."

McLoughlin wrote on November 24 that Indians frightened by the deaths had camped alongside the fort, so if they died the people at the fort could bury them. "Most reluctantly on our part we were obliged to drive them away," McLoughlin wrote, probably afraid that more of the sickness would spread into the fort.

Noted English botanist David Douglas, who first visited the fort as a guest in 1825 and later made it his headquarters for four years, also witnessed the fear and desolation resulting from the epidemic. He wrote from the mouth of the Columbia: "The

houses are empty and flocks of famished dogs are howling about while the dead bodies lie strewn in every direction on the sands of the river."

Fever and ague raged again in 1831, and McLoughlin received reports that fatalities among Indians along the Willamette River had been great. "There was no quinine in the country, the doctor [McLoughlin] being obliged to use dogwood root as a substitute," George Allan recalled. "From that

English botanist David Douglas made Fort Vancouver his headquarters for four years. He discovered 200 new species of plants while there, and sent seeds and seedlings back to England. The Douglas fir was named for him. Courtesy, Oregon Historical Society (neg. no. 19683)

DR. JOHN MCLOUGHLIN

Some associates of Dr. John McLoughlin called him "the Big Doctor." McLoughlin, chief factor of the Hudson's Bay Company at Fort Vancouver in fur-trading days, also has become known by a variety of other names such as the "White-Headed Eagle" and the "Father of the Oregon Country."

"A more indefatigable and enterprising man it would have been difficult to find," said Edward Ermatinger, a Hudson's Bay clerk. Joel Palmer, one of many visitors to the fort, concluded that McLoughlin "appears to be much of a gentleman." The Hudson's Bay governor, Sir George Simpson, found McLoughlin good-hearted, although of turbulent disposition, and believed he would "be radical in any country under any government."

McLoughlin's independent nature, or radical tendencies, as Simpson referred to them, did fit well with much of the job required of him. He needed to be innovative and decisive at times in maintaining the Hudson's Bay interests in its remote outposts in the Columbia River region. He

had to keep the Indian tribes under control, worked to exploit the fur business of the region, and developed trade with Russian Alaska, the Sandwich (Hawaiian) Islands, and California. McLoughlin also tried to deal diplomatically with an increasing number of Americans arriving in the Oregon country, where British and U.S. claims overlapped.

In trying to make his posts self-sufficient, McLoughlin was responsible, too, for some of the first activity of civilization in the region. He started a sawmill and an extensive farm near Vancouver, developed a large herd of cattle, started the first school in the Northwest, supervised some shipbuilding, and established a claim and mills at what is now Oregon City.

McLoughlin was born in 1784 near Riviere-du-Loup on the St. Lawrence River, Quebec, Canada, of Scottish, Irish, and French ancestry. He was educated in Canada, and was licensed to practice medicine and surgery. In 1803 McLoughlin joined the North West Company, which was in the fur business in Canada, and worked as a surgeon but soon proved adept as a

Dr. John McLoughlin (1784-1857) held power over a vast region as chief factor at Fort Vancouver. He retired from the Hudson's Bay Company in 1846 and died in Oregon City. Courtesy, Oregon Historical Society (neg. no. 67763)

fur trader. He was stationed for a considerable time in and near Fort William on Lake Superior.

When the North West Company merged with the Hudson's Bay Company in 1821, McLoughlin became a shock the Indians never recovered, and probably it was better for the whites, when settlers began to come in, as in former times it was dangerous to ascend the river in canoes without a strong crew, well armed."

Even with the epidemics, in 1832 the Indians were still numerous. They gathered near the fort on Sundays to dance in rings, a religious ceremony accompanied by singing. "As there were no Handels or Mozarts among them, the music was anything but charming to a delicate ear," Allan commented.

But the Indians couldn't hold back new arrivals. One adventurer who arrived late in 1832 was John Ball, who taught the fort's half-white, half-Indian youngsters from 1823 to 1833. McLoughlin was well satisfied with his efforts, and told Ball, "You will have the reputation of teaching the first Academy in Oregon." (At the time, land on both sides of the river was part of Oregon.)

Another American, Nathaniel Wyeth, visited as part of a small party in 1832. He described McLoughlin as "a fine old gentleman truly philanthropic in his ideas." Wyeth returned to the West in 1834, built Fort Hall in what is now Idaho, and established the short-lived Fort William on Sauvie Island. Three years later, Wyeth sold Fort Hall to the Hudson's Bay Company. Among travelers accompanying the Wyeth party across the country was

Hudson's Bay employee, and in 1824 he was chosen to head the Columbia district. Governor Simpson was his immediate superior but when Simpson left Fort Vancouver after its christening in March 1825, McLoughlin remained in sole charge.

McLoughlin supervised a striking aggregation of varied employees—like "a band of gypsies," as one observer described a party of sixty that set out from the fort in June 1828 on a punitive expedition against the Clallam Indians on Puget Sound. The party, sent out after the Clallams killed Alexander McKenzie and four of his men, consisted of Canadians, Iroquois and Chinook Indians, Kanakas (from the Sandwich Islands), with Scotch and English officers. The previous night the voyagers had celebrated with a regale, and the Iroquois staged a war dance.

Simpson also testified to the variety among company employees: "the prettiest congregation of nations, the nicest confusion . . . since the days of the tower of Babel." But McLoughlin was able to organize all the disparate individuals into a workable unit. A considerable number of employees lived with their families at Kanaka Village, southwest of the fort.

Efforts to build up trade in coastal vessels took up part of McLoughlin's time. Pioneering shipbuilding efforts at Vancouver were soon abandoned in favor of purchasing vessels elsewhere, or sending them from England.

In the 1830s McLoughlin was a host to a series of American visitors at Fort Vancouver, some of them missionaries. The number of new arrivals increased sharply in the 1840s, and McLoughlin aided many, even extending credit to a considerable number so they could make a start in the Willamette Valley. Higher officials in the Hudson's Bay Company were critical, but McLoughlin considered that he was faithful to the company as far as he could be, "without compromising my sense of justice or turning a deaf ear to the calls of humanity."

His last years at the fort were saddened by the death of his son, John McLoughlin, Jr., murdered in 1842 by employees at Fort Stikine, Canada, and the 1845 suicide of a son-in-law, William Glen Rae, who was in charge of Hudson's Bay trading efforts in the San Francisco Bay area. A breach between Simpson and McLoughlin was widened by the governor's failure to seek prosecution of the killers of young McLoughlin.

In 1846, McLoughlin left the fort and settled at Oregon City. He formally retired in 1849, applied the same year to become a U.S. citizen, and received his final citizenship papers in 1851. His Oregon City land was taken under a discriminatory section of the donation land law of 1850, but McLoughlin was allowed to continue to live there. In 1862, five years after McLoughlin's death, the Oregon Legislative Assembly conveyed the land claim, except Abernethy Island, to McLoughlin heirs for $1,000.

McLoughlin is buried on a hill near the falls at Oregon City with his wife Margaret, who was one-half or one-fourth Indian. The McLoughlins were survived by two daughters and a son. McLoughlin also had a son, Joseph, born to an earlier wife.

In 1907, a crowd suitably garbed for Sunday watches the Reverend Jones perform a baptism near a Battle Ground church that in later years developed into the Community United Methodist Church. Courtesy, The Columbian

Church, Classroom, and Communications

An oddly assorted congregation at Fort Vancouver assembled to hear the first sermon by a minister west of Fort Hall on September 28, 1834. Methodist minister Jason Lee jotted in his journal on that date:

A.M. Assayed to preach to a mixed congregation, English, French, Scotch, Irish, Indians, Americans, half breeds, Japanese &c, some of whom did not understand 5 words of English. Found it extremely difficult to collect my thoughts or find language to express them but am thankful that I have been permitted to plead the cause of God on this side of the Ry. Mountains where the banners of Christ were never before unfurled.

The Japanese mentioned probably were three seamen who had survived a shipwreck at Cape Flattery and stayed at the fort for a short time.

Lee wasn't the first to offer religious instruction in Vancouver. Before his arrival, the local population had, in earlier years, heard John McLoughlin read from the Church of England's *Book of Common Prayer.*

Catholic missionaries Francis Norbert Blanchet and Modeste Demers arrived at the fort in late 1838. A year later Blanchet, who would become the archbishop of Oregon, established his headquarters in the Willamette Valley, while Demers went to the Cowlitz area. They occasionally visited Vancouver to officiate at services, baptisms, weddings, and burials.

During the 1840s, all church services were conducted at the fort. A Catholic church was built there in 1845, and at that time the fort also contained an Owyhee church, where a former resident of the Sandwich (Hawaiian) Islands known as William or Kanaka William presided over religious ceremonies for the Kanakas.

Columbia City, as Vancouver was called from 1850 to 1855, developed into the region's cultural center, and congregations started to organize there. Traveling preachers frequently ministered to other congregations scattered far from the community's center. H.K. Hines, a Vancouver Methodist minister of the 1860s, described their routine:

Above: *"The finest taxi ride I ever had,"* said evangelist Aimee Semple McPherson after she rode on a Vancouver fire truck to the dedication of the Four Square Gospel Church at Eighteenth and Daniels on July 15, 1931. Courtesy, Ted Van Arsdol

Below: *Vancouver High School at 26th and Main was opened in 1913. The building was replaced in later years by a high-rise housing project after a futile effort by Robert Hidden and other residents to save the large auditorium for community events. Courtesy, Webfooters Postcard Club*

barracks, while on the outside people were standing upon window ledges, saw-horses, ladders and boxes in their eagerness to see what was going on."

One of the more unusual ministers living in Vancouver about the time of World War I and the 1920s was the Reverend A.D. Skaggs. A retired minister of the Christian Church, Skaggs was publicized as "the marrying parson of the Northwestern Gretna Green." At one point, Skaggs had married 6,193 persons, which he said was "probably a world's record." He had baptized 7,393 with his own hands, but had lost track of how many he had buried.

World War II greatly affected Vancouver churches, as war workers poured into the area. Nearly a quarter of a million people moved into the Portland-Vancouver metropolitan area from 1940 to 1945, and Vancouver churches reported congregation increases of one-fifth to two-thirds. Some of the churches added second services on Sundays. A United Church ministry was active in housing projects, and church schools were established there.

A dramatic change in the Vancouver area during the war was an influx of blacks. Several black churches were established, and there was at least one interdenominational, interracial church, located at Bagley Downs.

When the Kaiser Shipyard curtailed its activities in 1945, the population dropped, and churches de-

clined in attendance. Most blacks, lacking jobs after the Kaiser closure in 1946, moved away, many to Portland. At least two churches, New Hope Missionary Baptist and Vancouver Avenue Baptist, followed them to Portland.

Following World War II, new churches were constructed in Vancouver's outlying areas, as the population moved into the suburbs and new housing developments.

*   *   *

School days started in 1832 for Vancouver youngsters. One young pupil, Ranald MacDonald, left a brief memoir of how students fared with the first teacher, John Ball, at the Hudson's Bay Company fort: "I attended the school to learn my A.B.C.'s and English. The big boys had medals put over their necks if caught speaking French or Chinook and when school was out they had to remain and learn a task. I made no progress."

One early teacher, Richard Covington, began teaching at the fort in 1846. In 1848 he and his wife Ann moved to Fourth Plain, the present Orchards area, where they operated a boarding school. Their home, also used as a school, has been moved to 4201 Main Street in Vancouver and is the oldest existing school building in Clark County.

Education was a top civic priority when the town was established in the 1850s, but school terms were limited and students frequently dropped out. A high school was not established until 1888, occupying makeshift quarters until it moved into a new building in 1912.

Catholics sent their children to Providence Academy or Holy Angels College, and private schools

Top right: *Covington House near the end of North Main Street is the oldest school building still standing in Clark County. Dating from the mid-1840s, the structure was moved to Vancouver from its original site near Orchards in 1926. Courtesy, Ted Van Arsdol*

Right: *In 1896 Agnes Laurette Hill, later Mrs. J.J. Cairns, was the first official high school graduate of Providence Academy. The academy, which operated from 1857 to 1966, was one of the projects of the Sisters of Charity of Providence. Vancouver still has two Catholic schools. Courtesy,* The Columbian

Anton Young bought out Henry Weinhard's brewery interest in the mid-1860s and constructed this building adjoining the public square in 1867. Another brewery also was in business at the time. Young sold out in 1894 to the Gerlinger Company of Chicago. Courtesy, Clark County Museum

been burned over, there was still an abundance of trees, and woodcutting was a source of income for residents near steamboat landings along the Columbia River. This was a steady and increasing business for many years, as wood was hauled to the growing town. The Vancouver *Independent* reported in 1882 that seventy-five cords of wood had to be provided daily to steamboats getting wood at Vancouver, as well as for the people of the town and the garrison.

B.L. Morrison was one of the earliest wood products manufacturers, shipping large quantities of hoop poles to San Francisco. Louis Sohns and D.F. Schuele, who operated a cooper shop in the 1870s, also shipped items to San Francisco such as staves and barrel kegs.

McFarlane Brothers' logging camp in the Sara district northwest of Vancouver sent lumber by rail to nearby Lake River in 1898. Some of the camp's output went to Stella, below present-day Longview, to be used in forming huge oceangoing rafts. Courtesy, The Columbian

Paper has been turned out at a Camas mill since 1885. When this interior photo was taken about 1925, the paper plant was known as Crown-Willamette Pulp and Paper Company. Crown-Zellerbach now operates the mill. Courtesy, Oregon Historical Society (neg. no. 29892)

Lumber mills started in a small way. L.C. Palmer opened a small mill at Battle Ground in 1870, and later was in the mill business at Vancouver. The Lucia Mill was one of the first located along the waterfront.

Even with so much timber available, brick was in demand for construction. Lowell Mason Hidden and William Ginder entered this activity in 1871. A big order for Hidden and Ginder requested one million bricks in 1873 for the House of Providence, also known as Providence Academy, which later became a Vancouver landmark.

Work started near the end of 1883 to connect La Camas Lake by tunnel with the Columbia River at La Camas, thirteen miles east of Vancouver. In 1885 a paper mill was opened there, and the new town of La Camas, later Camas, thrived alongside the mill. The paper industry proved to be a durable business, eventually employing the most people of any enterprise in the county.

Hoping to bolster its lumber industry, Vancouver attempted to gain access to the timber-rich interior by building a railroad. The Vancouver, Klickitat and Yakima Railroad, Clark County's first, was incorporated in 1887. Work on the line began in 1888, and in 1889 the new Michigan Mill in Vancouver began sawing logs brought in by the railroad from the northeastern part of the county. The railroad was expected to be constructed across the Cascade Mountains to Yakima, but due to a lack of financing it never left the boundaries of the county.

Vancouver's waterfront was lively in the early 1890s, as products from the mills were brought in and loaded on commercial ships. An 1891-1892 directory of Vancouver industries listed five sawmills, two sash and door factories, a box factory, three brickyards, and the brewery. A streetcar line had been constructed in 1889, and real estate devel-

tainment in Vancouver as a theatrical staple. The most successful theater owner in Vancouver was John Kiggins. During World War I, Kiggins did good business with three theaters, patriotically named the Liberty, the U.S.A., and the American (formerly the Palace). Kiggins built the Castle in 1927 and the Kiggins, his last theater, in 1936. After World War II moviegoing became more of a pastime for the young, who now also turn out in great numbers for major rock concerts in Portland.

Dancing to the music of big bands was highly popular in the 1930s, 1940s, and early 1950s. Nationally known orchestras appeared frequently for dances at The Golden-Canopied Ballroom at Jantzen Beach. In Vancouver the Holcomb Ballroom, owned by local businessman Floyd Holcomb, was crowded at times with 2,000 dancers on Saturday nights during 1944-1945. Paul Howard of Orchards, who played in the band there, said 3,000 to 3,500 people sometimes crowded in and out on New Year's Eve and holidays. "It was noted as one of the largest ballrooms on the coast," he said.

Little theater, or community theater, which had gotten a foothold at the housing projects during

World War II, survived into the postwar era and became increasingly durable. The Vancouver Civic Theatre, active during the war, was revived for a short time in the 1950s. The Old Slocum House Theatre Company, specializing in plays of the Victorian era, was established in 1965 by Hermine Decker, a Clark College drama instructor. She retired from Clark in 1971, and the theater group moved the following year into an old restored home.

Carolyn and Keith Neubauer, Bruce and Joyce Siau, and others produced large-scale musicals in school auditoriums as the Peanut Gallery Theatre Company, organized in 1972. The Clark County Community Players (later the Encore Players), the Clark College Theatre, and the Northwest Theatre of the Deaf have also been active.

Events that continue to attract large crowds are the Fourth of July celebration at Fort Vancouver National Historic Site; the Clark County Fair, with nationally known country and pop music entertainers; the Vancouver Sausage Festival, a money-raising event for St. Joseph Catholic School; and the Miss Washington Pageant.

Opposite page: *A large bathing pool was one of four pools drawing funseekers to Jantzen Beach. The amusement park, opened in 1928, reached its peak of popularity during World War II. Jantzen Knitting Mills promoted the park on Hayden Island to help sell swimming suits. Courtesy, Jantzen Beach Center*

Left: *Cancan dancers added verve to a 1955 pageant, part of a week-long Cenaqua celebration commemorating the establishment of Fort Vancouver. Other big historical celebrations in Vancouver included a centennial in 1925 and a 1939 pageant depicting the arrival of Catholic missionaries in 1838. Courtesy,* The Columbian

Below: *Troops from Vancouver Barracks relax at the Log Cabin Saloon at 502 Main Street shortly before World War I. Among downtown businesses, the Log Cabin, with a cabin exterior, was one of the most distinctive. The Evergreen Hotel now occupies the site of the saloon, which was a casualty of Prohibition. Courtesy, Clark County Museum*

While he was at Vancouver in 1852-1853, Lieutenant Ulysses S. Grant tried potato raising, cattle shipping, and other ventures to supplement his army pay. He was homesick for his family, however, and temporarily left the army after an unhappy stay at his next post in Northern California. Courtesy, National Archives

Notables of 140 Years

The military contained some of the brightest stars among early Vancouver residents, as numerous officers stationed at the barracks in the 1850s received big promotions in the Civil War. Later in Vancouver's history civilians won acclaim or notice in a wide range of activities, but for many years the civilian population was not large, and the tally of prominent individuals was weighted heavily with military personnel.

B.L.E. Bonneville, made famous by Washington Irving's *The Adventures of Captain Bonneville, U.S.A.,* was a commanding officer of the barracks from 1853 to 1855. At the time he was a lieutenant colonel of the Fourth Infantry.

Most other officers stationed at Vancouver in the 1850s were not so well known at the time, but fame was thrust on many of them during the Civil War. Franz Feinler, a chaplain with the First Infantry Regiment at Vancouver in 1911, compiled a list of 175 officers connected with barracks history before August 1, 1861, and found that 66 reached the rank of brigadier general or higher.

One officer who gained public acclaim was Ulysses S. Grant, stationed at Vancouver from 1852 to 1853. He went on to command the Union forces in the later stages of the Civil War and was President of the United States from 1869 to 1877.

Another Union general, George McClellan, had led a railroad surveying party out of Vancouver in the mid-1850s. He was the Democratic Presidential candidate in 1864.

Rufus Ingalls, a quartermaster at the barracks when it was initially constructed and one of Vancouver's first Masons, served as chief quartermaster of the Army of the Potomac.

Of the twenty-nine Vancouver officers siding with the Confederate states, William Wing Loring probably had the most colorful career. Loring, who had lost an arm in the Mexican War, was a colonel when he led the Mounted Riflemen across the plains to Vancouver. After fighting for the South, he served in the Egyptian Army as a major general and wrote a book about his experiences there.

A series of well-known Indian fighters were commanding officers of the Department of the Columbia after the Civil War. These included O.O. Howard, Nelson Miles, and John Gibbon.

CHAPTER   IV

Above: *Lieutenant Philip H. Sheridan was involved in Indian fighting in the Yakima area while based at Vancouver. In 1856 he took troops on the steamboat* Belle *to meet an Indian attack at The Cascades. During the Civil War, Sheridan became a cavalry commander. In 1883 he was named commanding general of the U.S. Army. Courtesy, National Archives*

Below: *Rufus Ingalls served at the barracks from 1849 to 1853 and from 1856 to 1860 as deputy Pacific division quartermaster. Ingalls gained major general rank during the Civil War in the quartermasters. Courtesy, National Archives*

Above: *While Brigadier General William Harney was department commanding officer at Vancouver, he became embroiled in a San Juan Islands dispute which the British called "The Pig War." A Vancouver school, hill, and neighborhood were named for Harney. Courtesy, National Archives*

Below: *During Brigadier General O.O. Howard's tenure as Department of the Columbia commander from 1874 to 1881, troops had to be sent out to subdue Chief Joseph's Nez Perce Indians (1877) and the Bannocks (1878). Courtesy, National Archives*

Brigadier General Nelson Miles headed some public events in Vancouver, such as Memorial Day services in 1882. During the Spanish-American War Miles became commander of the U.S. Army. A Vancouver newspaper called him "the handsomest soldier in the Army." Courtesy, National Archives

Alfred Sully, whose story is told in the book *No Tears for the General,* was commanding officer at the barracks until his death in 1879. He had fought against the Sioux in the 1860s.

Other Vancouver officers sought adventure away from the battlefield. George Goethals, later in charge of construction of the Panama Canal, and Frederick Schwatka, noted Arctic explorer, were lieutenants at Vancouver in the 1880s.

While commanding the Fourteenth Infantry Regiment, Colonel Thomas M. Anderson had one of the longest tenures among commanding officers of Vancouver Barracks. He was barracks CO most of the time from 1886 until 1898, when he was named brigadier general in charge of the first U.S. expeditionary force sailing from San Francisco to Manila.

Many soldiers stationed at or passing through Vancouver eventually settled in Clark County. John Betzing, who served in the Prussian Army and, later, the Fourteenth Infantry, worked as a tailor in civilian life and died in Vancouver in 1904.

In the post cemetery, tombstones call attention to the final resting places of several Medal of Honor recipients: among them are Moses Williams, a black sergeant who was cited for a battle with Indians in New Mexico; and Herman Pfisterer, a U.S. Army musician who aided wounded men under fire in Cuba in 1898.

Among Vancouver's famous civilians was C.W. Slocum, one of the city's most successful merchants for three decades. In the 1860s he operated stores at Walla Walla, Lewiston, and Boise and freighted goods to outlying Northwest military installations.

Louis Sohns, another notable of the 1800s, was a businessman, mayor, organizer of the first water system, and pioneer banker.

The Hidden family began making its impact with the arrival in the 1860s of Lowell Hidden, who became involved in an array of activities. He operated a brickyard and a flour and feed mill, helped organize the Vancouver, Klickitat and Yakima Railroad, and operated the Columbia Hotel at Third and Main in the 1890s with his brothers Oliver and Arthur.

Lowell's son, W. Foster Hidden, was a leading businessman as well as a farmer. At his death *The Columbian* editorialized that he "accumulated many worldly goods, but his personal pattern of living remained unchanged." W. Foster's son Robert continued with the brickyard, real estate, and other interests and was a leading authority on local history.

Some women were also prominent in the early years. Mother Joseph, who arrived in Vancouver in 1856 and headed the Sisters of Charity of Providence, was an outstanding humanitarian. According to St. James Historical Society president Victoria Ransom, Mother Joseph "started the first hospital [non-military] here in Vancouver, as well as the first orphanage, home for the homeless and aged, and a place for the insane ... These were all firsts for Washington Territory."

The sister also founded hospitals, schools, and orphanages in other Northwest communities, frequently financing these efforts with trips to mining regions to solicit funds. Many of the institutions she established are still in existence.

Mother Joseph was skilled as a carpenter and was also an architect, designing the House of Provi-

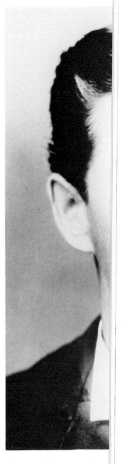

James Troup gained
steamboat Vancouve
Later he was in char
and supervised its st
pervised the design
Courtesy, Oregon H

1010 Esther Stre
offices of Bernar
Michael Langsdo
a former Clark C

F.W. Leadbett
industrialists of t
Portland *Oregon*
gone to Camas t
the early 1900s s
ities in the Cam
Leadbetter Comp
made big news ir
opened the Colu
"This has been
Leadbetter said.

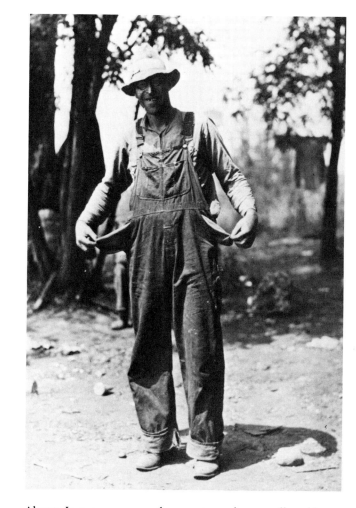

Above: *In one way or another, most people were affected by the Great Depression. One penniless individual of the era was this transient, who turned his pockets inside out for the photographer at a hobo camp at the north end of the Interstate Bridge. Courtesy, Oregon Historical Society (neg. no. 12881)*

the Vancouver water system and development of Lewisville Park on the East Fork of the Lewis River were among the larger jobs.

The largest project in the region was Bonneville Dam, built during the mid-1930s at the town of North Bonneville, forty miles east of Vancouver. President Roosevelt spoke at the dam on September 28, 1937, and pressed a button that activated the first generator. On the same day he dedicated the WPA-built Timberline Lodge at Mount Hood in Oregon and stopped briefly at the Vancouver train depot before continuing on to Seattle.

Better times returned gradually. Then, on December 7, 1941, Japanese planes attacked Pearl Harbor, triggering America's entry into World War II. This was the most disruptive event so far for Vancouver.

Henry Kaiser, previously involved in dam construction, established a shipyard at Vancouver in early 1942, a short distance upstream from the Interstate Highway Bridge. Edgar Kaiser was general manager of the yard and two additional yards in Portland, building ships for the war effort.

Employment built up steadily and reached a peak of more than 38,000 in December 1943. Hiring was limited largely to men at first, but as personnel shortages developed increasing numbers of women were employed. By November 1943, women totaled more than 10,000 on Kaiser's payroll. "The first women who came out were a novelty and the men didn't think they would last long," said Hugh Gray, an assembly building foreman. "It was dirty work and they wore big heavy overalls for protection.

Below: *Ships were shaping up in a dozen ways at the Kaiser yard, a short distance south of the Evergreen Highway, at the time of this wartime aerial photo, circa 1944. Courtesy, Oregon Historical Society (neg. no. 35797)*

EDGAR KAISER

Industrialist Henry Kaiser's zest for the future "made him impatient with those who dwell on the past," said his son, Edgar Kaiser. The same comment might have been made about Edgar, whose own busy role as Kaiser heir left him little time for leisurely pursuits.

Edgar Kaiser's headquarters during most of his later years was Oakland, California. But one of his most memorable jobs was heading Kaiser activities in Vancouver and Portland during World War II. The Kaiser Company operated three shipyards in the area—Swan Island and Oregon Shipbuilding at St. Johns (both on the Willamette River), and a Vancouver shipyard on the Columbia upstream from the Interstate Bridge. A total of about 97,000 men and women were employed at the three yards during the peak; 38,000 worked at Vancouver.

Edgar Kaiser's family lived in a Vancouver home on Overlook Drive with a view of the Vancouver yard and some worker housing. Not far away, in an area south of McLoughlin Heights, was Kaiser's Northern Permanente Hospital, serving the company's workers in the metropolitan area.

A few miles downriver from Kaiser's home, many Kaiser workers were housed in Oregon's second largest city, Vanport, a wartime project built by Six Companies, in which Henry Kaiser was a leader. Many thousands of Kaiser workers resided in other housing projects; the largest of these on the Vancouver side of the Columbia was McLoughlin Heights, occupying several miles of upland near Edgar Kaiser's home.

Edgar Kaiser, a native of Spokane, had been well prepared for the construction challenges he faced at Vancouver. He had worked in construction camps as a youth when his father was gaining experience and a reputation as a construction chief.

"You find your key men by piling work on them," Henry Kaiser said, and his son apparently was no exception to Henry's rule.

In the early 1930s, Edgar Kaiser worked on the construction of natural gas lines in the West and Midwest. Later he was a shift superintendent at Boulder Dam, when his father was executive committee chairman of the Six Companies, the dam contractor.

In 1934, Edgar Kaiser arrived on the Columbia River as administrative manager for the Columbia Construction Co., which had the contract for the Bonneville Dam, forty miles east of Vancouver. The company was composed of a majority of the owners who were building Boulder Dam. Kaiser, who worked at Bonneville until 1938, later called Bonneville Dam the most difficult job ever attempted by the Kaiser people. One setback at Bonneville was the river's destruction of a cofferdam.

An even larger dam, the Grand Coulee, was next. Henry Kaiser was manager of Consolidated Builders, Inc., the Grand Coulee contractor, and Edgar Kaiser was project manager from 1938 to 1941.

The Japanese attack on Pearl Harbor on December 7, 1941, altered the nation's priorities. One immediate need was the construction of ships. The Kaiser organization's construction know-how proved transferable to ships, and in a short time Kaiser was operating seven West Coast shipyards located at Vancouver, Portland, and Richmond, California.

Near the end of 1942, Edgar Kaiser was named Portland's first citizen of the year. Two years earlier, Portland's largest payroll had been 1,100; the three Kaiser yards already had 76,000 employees when Kaiser, general manager of the yards, was named first citizen.

The Kaiser yards used special methods of prefabrication and construction and greatly reduced the length of time required for shipbuilding. During World War II, Kaiser's yards built about 30 percent of all U.S. merchant ships, plus fifty small aircraft carriers. The Kaiser organization also was involved in other types of war work for the U.S. government.

Shortly after the end of the war, Edgar Kaiser left Vancouver. He was president and director of the Kaiser Motors Corp. in 1945-1946, and later was involved in other activities. He was named president of Kaiser Industries Corp. in 1956, and succeeded his father as chairman of Kaiser Aluminum, Kaiser Cement, and Kaiser Steel in 1959. Edgar Kaiser was a strong supporter of private enterprise abroad, and his organization was a contractor on big projects overseas.

At the time of Kaiser's death in December 1981 in California, the most notable reminder of the Kaiser presence in the Vancouver area was the Kaiser medical plan, covering 250,000 persons in the Vancouver-Portland area and Salem. The medical plan had evolved from Henry Kaiser's efforts to provide health facilities in the 1930s for his dam and pipeline workers.

Edgar Kaiser was general manager of the Vancouver Shipyard and two yards in Portland. He later took over Kaiser's diverse postwar activities. Courtesy, Kaiser Industries

Warren Weber designed the distinctively shaped First Congregational Church, United Church of Christ, which was built in Hazel Dell in the early 1960s. Construction of suburban churches was extensive following World War II. Photo by Holloway McCluskey

These logs will be processed into plywood and other wood products at the mills of Ft. Vancouver Plywood. The company is located in the port industrial area, not far from where Standifer shipyard's steel and wooden ships were launched during World War I. Photo by Holloway McCluskey

Mount St. Helens has continued to erupt occasionally since May 18, 1980, when an eruption blasted off its top and left fifty-six people dead or missing. Copyright, James Lee/EARTH IMAGES

Steam ferries developed a good business hauling vehicles and passengers across the Columbia River between Vancouver and Portland. The City of Vancouver, *shown here circa 1913, was the last of a series of such ferries. Courtesy, Ted Van Arsdol*

Shifting Scenes

L oops and swirls of roadway, some elevated, cluster at the north end of the Interstate bridges of Vancouver, extending as far north as the old Evergreen Hotel, once considered to be in the middle of downtown. The interchanges carry relentless traffic, tens of thousands of cars and trucks daily, that heads south toward Portland and the Willamette Valley, swings east toward Camas along the Columbia River, and streams north toward Hazel Dell, Woodland, and Seattle. The interchanges have displaced most of what was once the lower part of downtown, below Fifth Street.

On a gray pillar on the river side of the loops near the bridge, an engraved message conveys the attitude of the bridge builders of 1917. It quotes John Ruskin, English writer and art critic:

Therefore, when we build, let us think that we build forever . . . Let it be such work as our descendants will thank us for, and let us think, as we lay stone on stone, that a time is to come when those stones will be held sacred because our hands have touched them, and that men will say as they look upon the labor and wrought substance of them, 'See! This our fathers did for us.'

If Ruskin could see the work of the modern-day builders in the Vancouver area, successors of the people who constructed the first interstate highway span, he probably would be quite impressed. He would be intrigued by the Vancouver and Jantzen Beach shopping malls, housing a total of 224 shops and stores, and by the tide of motor vehicles providing access to these centers during shopping hours. He probably would be astounded by the amounts of money spent on routes for today's motorized traffic—$175 million for the Glenn Jackson Bridge alone, which ties together the Washington and Oregon sections of Interstate 205.

Many millions also have been spent since World War II in enlarging and improving Highway 5 in the Vancouver area. This is the major north-south route linking the Puget Sound area with Portland, the Willamette Valley, and California. But highways, bridges, and shopping malls are just a part of Vancouver's extensive alterations.

Motor vehicle transportation, permitting the pop-

CHAPTER

VI

GREATER VANCOUVER CHAMBER OF COMMERCE

In April 1890 the Vancouver Chamber of Commerce Company filed articles of incorporation with James A. Snodgrass, the Clark County auditor. The stated objective was to buy land and construct and maintain a building. The corporation's capital stock was to be $25,000, divided into 500 shares of $50 each, and its life span was to be 50 years. Seven trustees were named: P.C. Kauffman, W. Byron Daniels, E.L. Canby, L.M. Hidden, Lynn B. Clough, S.M. Beard, and P.C. McFarlane.

In 1927 the Vancouver Chamber of Commerce embarked on a project that was to leave its mark on city history. It decided to build "a new and modern hotel" at the corner of Fifth and Main streets. The organization hired a professional fund raiser who set up four sales division teams. A large sign went up downtown listing individual names and daily money totals raised. On May 14, the goal was reached—$143,800. Thus, the historic Evergreen Hotel was born in 1928.

Four years later chamber directors obtained a loan of $100,000 from the Reconstruction Finance Corporation to assist the Port of Vancouver in substantial dock construction im-

A 60-foot owl and pussycat surrounded by clowns entertained Vancouver residents as part of a chamber parade of giant balloons.

provements to help develop port capacity and relieve unemployment. The following year the association organized civic and industrial groups into a strong force to carry out the provisions of the National Industrial Recovery Act. In 1936 the chamber led arbitration efforts that settled a WPA strike.

That same year the Salmon Creek Grange threatened to boycott all Vancouver merchants if they cooperated with the city in installing parking meters. Chamber members voted against meters more than two to one. The year 1936 also brought a battle with the United States Census Bureau, which refused to count residents of the Vancouver Barracks as citizens of the city, leaving out 2,000 soldiers who had been in the 1930 count. Approximately $110,000 per year from the state was at stake. Justice prevailed after the chamber and Mayor Al Stanley showed that troops at the Presidio in San Francisco were counted as residents.

In the 1950s a five-year battle by the chamber to win freight rate parity with Oregon was won, resulting in annual savings of nearly $40,000 to industries. In 1958 the organization spearheaded the effort to create a Regional Planning Commission. Members also met with Congressman Russell Mack to request toll-free status for the Interstate Bridge and a

In 1926 this van, complete with pull-down shades, heralded the merits of Vancouver and Clark County.

35-foot channel to the port docks.

In 1970 the chamber opposed a local sales tax authorization bill by the state. The year 1976 brought active negotiations by the organization for zone changes to bring Tektronix to Clark County, and business and occupation tax equity at the city level. In addition, chamber members were actively involved in the port's Vancouver Lake restoration project.

In 1981 the association helped kick off the Downtown Boosters, and a brand-name preference poll was taken in the core area, financed by downtown businesses, the chamber, and *The Columbian*. That same year the organization established a Small Business Council to provide dialogue with the Washington, D.C., congressional delegation.

In the 1980s the Greater Vancouver Chamber of Commerce sponsored world trade seminars, opened a travel information center, started a Clark County Visitors and Convention Bureau, established an annual Christmas breakfast for people in need, and began a series of Business After Hours networking sessions with major businesses as hosts. Membership in 1986, nearly 100 years after its inception, reached 1,175.

BLAIR, SCHAEFER, HUTCHISON, WYNNE, POTTER & HORTON

Through most of the past century the principals of this prestigious firm or their forebears have been influential in Vancouver and the State of Washington. Total commitment to service to the community is a working attitude that has produced a history-making record of achievement.

The partnership of Robert Schaefer's grandfather, Donald McMaster, and Charles Hall was established in the early 1900s followed by McMaster, Hall and (Louis) Schaefer. When McMaster went on the bench, it became Schaefer and Hall, then Schaefer and Scheiber, then Scheiber and (Bob) Schaefer, then Scheiber, Schaefer & Wynne. When Scheiber became a judge in January 1965, Schaefer and Wynne merged with Hutchison and Blair (which had been formed in 1953) to establish Blair, Schaefer, Hutchison & Wynne.

Donald C. Blair, whose great-uncle was in the first state legislature and whose father was an attorney active in Clark County community and Republican party affairs, graduated from Washington State University and the University of Washington Law School. Blair, a retired colonel, USAR, was admitted to the bar in 1949.

Robert McMaster Schaefer is the son of Louis Schaefer and the former Mildred McMaster, whose father was Judge Donald McMaster. His father had been chairman of the Democratic party and was an outstanding attorney in Clark County. A law graduate of Willamette University, Schaefer was admitted to the bar in 1955 and served as a deputy prosecutor. In 1958 he was elected a state representative. Although he was elected Speaker of the House in 1964, Schaefer decided not to seek reelection in 1966 so he could devote time and energy to family, law practice, and community.

David C. Hutchison grew up in Proebstel where his parents owned a general store. A law graduate of the University of Washington, he was admitted to the bar in 1950. Following law school, he served as a clerk for Supreme Court Justice Thomas E. Grady. He held positions as president of the Clark County Bar Association from 1952 to 1953; as city attorney from 1951 to 1955; and as chairman of the Vancouver School Board in 1971-1972. He is a retired lieutenant colonel in the Judge Advocate General's Corps, USAR.

John F. Wynne, who was born in Wigan, England, grew up in Connecticut. While attending Georgetown University Law School in Washington, D.C., he worked for Senator Henry Jackson. Wynne came west as an attorney with the Bonneville Power Administration and became city attorney for Vancouver. He has represented the Clark County Public Utility District since September 1965.

Hugh Potter, University of Oregon, joined the firm in 1974; James D.

Hollow blocks, created on-site at the corner of 11th and Franklin, formed the structure of this former banker's home built in 1905. There are two fireplaces, and two staircases (one was for servants).

Horton, Gonzaga University, joined in 1976. Charles R. Cusack, Jr., Lewis and Clark, joined in the late 1970s. Other partners are John R. Potter, Lewis and Clark Law School; Donald Russo, St. Louis University; and Wayne W. Nelson, Lewis and Clark.

Clients of Blair, Schaefer, Hutchison, Wynne, Potter & Horton include Clark County PUD, Community First Federal Savings, Genstar Development, Inc., Hewlett-Packard Company, Kyocera Northwest, LaValley Industrial Plastics, Inc., MacKay & MacDonald, Reidel International, SEH America, Inc., and Seattle-First National Bank.

Partners in the firm (from left, rear) are James D. Horton, John R. Potter, Wayne W. Nelson, Hugh H. Potter, Charles R. Cusack, Jr., and Donald Russo. Seated (from left) are Donald C. Blair, David C. Hutchison, John F. Wynne, and Robert M. Schaefer.

CLARK PUBLIC UTILITY DISTRICT

An aerial view of the Ed Fischer Operations Center, named in honor of a longtime PUD Commissioner who retired in 1984 after 20 years of service.

Clark Public Utility District is a consumer-owned electric and water utility created in 1938 by a vote of Clark County citizens. The PUD grew out of citizen frustration with the high rates and poor service offered by the two investor-owned utilities that served the county at that time. Formation of the PUD was a logical step, as a consumer-owned utility is designed to give the public a voice in policies and operations.

The effort to form the PUD was led by a committee of business and labor representatives, and members of the Grange. Earlier attempts to form a PUD had failed in 1934 and again in 1936. Those years saw numerous battles between supporters of both consumer-owned and investor-owned utilities throughout the Pacific Northwest, as residents in much of the region increasingly demanded a greater role in decisions affecting their electrical future. An important factor was the construction of the Bonneville and Grand Coulee dams,

and the formation of the Bonneville Power Administration to sell power produced at the dams. The concept of building the dams was the brainchild of President Franklin D. Roosevelt. Constructed to provide much-needed jobs during the Depression, they brought significant benefits to the region, including flood control, irriga-

The PUD's Electric Center serves as administrative headquarters for the utility.

tion, and most important, low-cost power.

Though the PUD was formed in 1938, it was nearly four years before the first kilowatt hour of electricity was sold. That occurred in 1942, when a contract was signed with the Vancouver Housing Authority to provide power to several wartime housing projects constructed in conjunction with the Kaiser Shipyard. The PUD outbid the two private companies to win the contract to serve the projects with power purchased from BPA.

Meanwhile, negotiations continued with the investor-owned utilities for the PUD's purchase of their facilities. There was little progress, and eventually the price was set by the courts. In 1945 a federal court in Tacoma set a price of $801,000 on facilities of Portland General Electric. The PUD took possession in January 1946, giving it about 4,500 new customers. The remaining private utility, Northwestern Electric (now Pacific Power), cut commercial and industrial rates, and the PUD followed suit. A bitter competitive battle between the two utilities followed, and customers switched back and forth. Again the question of public versus private power became an election issue, with a statewide anti-PUD measure put on the ballot and supported by private electric companies. The measure was defeated by a large margin.

It took until November 1947 for a superior court jury to place a value on Northwestern Electric properties, and it was February of the following year before the PUD completed acquisition of the system for $4.8 million. As a result, the PUD became the county's only electric utility, serving about 22,000 customers.

The next few years brought about a comprehensive modernization program that had been deferred during World War II. However, disaster struck in 1950, when a January sleet storm leveled much of the system. The PUD borrowed $500,000 to rebuild it and raised rates 7 percent to finance the six-year notes. Later that year work was begun on the PUD water system in Hazel Dell, which began providing service the following

Construction of Bonneville Dam during the 1930s was one of many factors that led to the formation of the PUD.

A portion of PUD's fleet at the old operations center. Photo circa 1955

year to 347 customers in the area of Highway 99 and 78th Street.

In 1951 the PUD launched a program to provide modern street lighting in downtown Vancouver. In subsequent years this led to new systems in Camas, Washougal, Battle Ground, Ridgefield, La Center, Yacolt, and Amboy. The utility also spearheaded passage of a rural street lighting bill in 1953 and organized the state's first three lighting districts.

Throughout the 1950s and 1960s the PUD and utilities in other areas actively promoted installation of electric heating systems. Clark PUD was so successful that electricity became virtually the only choice for heating in new homes and businesses. That trend continues. The marketing effort made sense because of the availability of surplus power—the more electricity sold through existing facilities, the lower the unit cost became. That resulted in more efficient use of PUD facilities and lower rates. The choice of electricity for heating continued through the 1970s and 1980s. Today about 80 percent of the homes and businesses in Clark County use electricity for heating, as electricity has proven to be clean, safe, efficient, and economical.

In 1962 another major storm created

At the PUD Water Utility, monitoring water quality is a priority.

Round tub files contained billing records prior to 1973 and the introduction of computerization to the system.

havoc countywide. The Columbus Day storm left virtually every home and business without electricity, and PUD crews worked continuous shifts of up to 40 hours at a time restoring service.

The PUD has been active in economic development over the years. In 1963 the utility and the Port of Vancouver formed the Clark County Industrial Bureau, with the purpose of actively seeking new industries. Though the bureau no longer exists, the PUD continues to work closely with developers and organizations, including area chambers of commerce, to assist in further development of the county.

Over the years the PUD has been a consistent leader in the utility industry, forging new programs and policies to meet the needs of its customers. In 1968, for example, it decided that all future subdivisions would be served with underground distribution systems. That proved to be a well-timed and popular decision since it preceded Clark County's building boom of the 1970s. As a

result, nearly half of the PUD's residential customers now have underground service, a desirable feature for home buyers.

The 1962 Columbus Day storm caused major damage to the PUD system and left nearly all its customers without power.

After more than three decades of plentiful, low-cost power, the Pacific Northwest faced drought conditions in 1973. The PUD joined other utilities in taking emergency action to promote conservation. A 7-percent savings was achieved through an aggressive public information program—an extension of the PUD's ongoing activities to promote the efficient use of electricity. The Gold Medallion Home program, adopted in 1958, had established insulation guidelines to increase home comfort and efficiency. Similar programs continued during the 1970s and 1980s to assist home buyers in selecting energy-efficient homes.

Other conservation programs included water heater wrapping and the PUD's Energy Buy-Back program, which has provided more than one-third of elegible home owners with insulation and other weatherization improvements. The PUD also provides innovative educational programs that keep customers aware of up-to-date advice on energy use and products.

Clark PUD customers have been fortunate in receiving excellent service at electricity rates that have contin-

staggered six-year terms by the voters of Clark County. Commissioners meet weekly in an open public forum to set policies and discuss issues and operations. A citizens' rate advisory committee meets to study and recommend rate policy. In addition, customers can "talk back" to the PUD using a special section on customer payment stubs. One in 10 payments includes comments, ranging from name and address corrections to opinions on major issues.

This customer relations program allows the PUD to offer new and improved services and has resulted in numerous innovations in the area of customer service. In an era of increasing public dissatisfaction with decreasing service and rising costs, the PUD has successfully bucked the trend by maintaining stable rates and, at the same time, increasing service.

Clark PUD is poised to meet the future needs of its customers. Employee productivity rates very high compared to other electric utilities. Increased productivity has been aided by the addition of automation in nearly all aspects. Significant improvements came from computer enhancements in customer service, which have dramatically reduced paperwork and improved performance.

Another innovation uses a microcomputer to monitor and control substations. Installation of the substation control system will also result in improved security throughout the electric system.

The 1980s have seen the evolution of a leaner, more efficient Clark Public Utility District—the result of years of tough decisions and hard work. These changes have prepared the PUD to meet the future needs of Clark County. The PUD continues to provide quality service while holding rates stable—and at a level that is the envy of people in other parts of the country.

Modern-day PUD line crews at work.

ued to be about one-half the national average. The transmission and distribution system has been carefully designed to provide high reliability. The PUD premise is to provide electric service that customers can count on being available. Most of the system is built using "looped" transmission and distribution lines, which allow for much higher reliability by providing two sources of power to most of the utility's service area.

As a consumer-owned utility, the PUD stays in touch with its customers. Policies are set by a three-member board of commissioners, elected to

VANCOUVER FEDERAL SAVINGS BANK

The Vancouver Savings and Loan Association building on the northeast corner of Main Street and 10th (now Evergreen Boulevard) was dedicated on November 6, 1929.

In 1919 money was loaned by commercial banks and local citizens of means, but was not widely available. There was a great need to provide a source of home loan capital. In response to that demand, Vancouver Savings and Loan Association was organized.

John B. Atkinson and Harry R. Porter were two of Vancouver's leading real estate and insurance agents following World War I. Atkinson, known to his friends as "J.B.," also worked as a loan broker and investor for local parties. It was in the capacity of investment broker that Atkinson was given the opportunity to establish the first savings and loan association in Clark County.

One day in 1919 Oscar Albert "O.A." Johnson, a conductor of the Spokane, Portland and Seattle Railroad's Portland to Spokane route, called on Atkinson. Johnson had a $4,500 check of his mother's that he wanted invested wisely. The check was drawn on a Minnesota savings and loan association, and Atkinson's curiosity was piqued.

Although the associations, first called "friendly societies" and later "building societies," had been established since the 1800s, it wasn't until states began regulating them about the turn of the century that they began to come into prominence. In 1919 there were four commercial banks in Vancouver, but there was not one savings association in the

From left to right: Bob Wilson, mayor of Vancouver; Dr. A.P. Ryan, VanFed director; Ray Woolf, VanFed director; and Tom Carver, executive vice-president, break ground for the headquarters building at 1205 Broadway in 1961.

entire county.

On January 22, 1920, the articles of incorporation of Vancouver Savings and Loan were filed with the Secretary of State. The nine board members were J.B. Atkinson; his partner, Harry R. Porter, who, as executive secretary/treasurer, was the first managing officer responsible for conducting the business affairs of the association; Atkinson's conductor friend O.A. Johnson; C.W. Ryan, a lumberman and first president of the association; druggist Miles R. Smith; two bankers, W.S. Short and Roy Hesseltine; and two dentists, Dr. A.P. Ryan and Dr. N.J. Taylor. Their attorney was William C. "Billy" Bates, who also became a board member in 1929 and served until 1973, when he became director emeritus.

Atkinson and Porter were very generous with the new business. Vancouver Savings and Loan's first headquarters was in their office at 112 West Sixth Street, and they met the payroll during the first ten years of operation.

Board minutes of 1921 indicate that the August meeting was canceled because of a conflict with a Rotary Club gathering; monthly rent to Atkinson and Porter was $37.50; and

the board felt the need for a safe and bought Atkinson and Porter's for $100.

On November 6, 1929, Vancouver Savings and Loan dedicated its new building on the northeast corner of Main and 10th (now Evergreen Boulevard). That same year J.B. Atkinson passed away, and on December 30 his son Neal was appointed to the board. Neal also took over his father's insurance business, known later as Atkinson, Millar & Ingalls. He served on the board for 52 years.

The thrift business in the 1930s was not easy. Through the trying years of the Great Depression, Vancouver Savings and Loan remained strong. It was the only savings and loan association in Vancouver to pay dividends regularly throughout the Depression.

During the early 1930s new federal laws were passed, and Vancouver Savings and Loan was the only association in Clark County to be accepted for direct 100-percent conversion from a state to a federal charter in 1934, two years after the Federal Home Loan Bank System was established. This action also resulted in its first name change to Vancouver Federal Savings and Loan Association.

Economic growth continued throughout World War II, although during the war the institution invested more than half its assets in government bonds to help the war effort.

Vancouver Federal Savings and Loan continued to grow—and with it emerged a thriving community, proud of its new homes, businesses, and schools. The expansion of the 1950s and 1960s created so many customers that the association also needed to grow. In 1960 its first branch office opened in McLoughlin Heights. Plans for a new home office at its present location at 1205 Broadway were developed, and on August 21, 1961, the new headquarters was dedicated.

As the outlying communities in

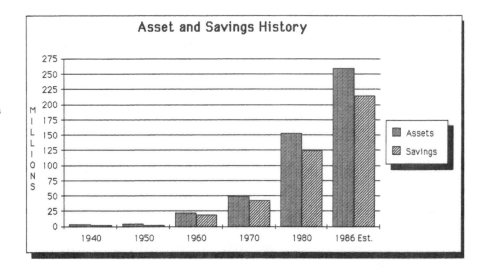

Clark County grew, Vancouver Federal responded to their needs by opening branch offices. In 1965 the Camas-Washougal office opened, followed by branches in Minnehaha in 1973, Hazel Dell in 1975, and Orchards in 1976.

The economic turbulence of the early 1980s sent a shock wave through the nation's financial institutions. High interest rates and the accompanying recession forced the closure or merger of many banks and savings and loans. Vancouver Federal Savings and Loan emerged from this difficult period as a strong institution, capable of meeting the financial needs of its customers.

Several changes were made that allowed Vancouver Federal to survive during this period. In order to provide more direct management capable of reacting more quickly to an ever-changing economic environment, the association converted from a managing officer to a full-time chief executive officer, the first of whom was Loren Means.

In 1985 the federal charter was amended to create new powers and offer a variety of banking products and services. The institution's name also was changed to Vancouver Federal Savings Bank, in order to reflect the expanded role. A new logo was

created, still using a Fort Vancouver theme, but also incorporating the institution's nickname, VanFed, which many of its customers had been using anyway.

Today Vancouver Federal Savings Bank is prospering. With new powers and new opportunities it can provide larger and more diverse lines of financial products. Beginning in early 1986 VanFed became available to its customers through Automatic Teller Machines (ATMs) at nine 7-Eleven stores in Clark County. It also is a member of the Exchange network, which provides customers with access to more than 5,000 ATM locations throughout the United States and Canada. The early 1980s also moved the institution into position as the leading real estate lender in Clark County.

VanFed's mission has been to build on the integrity and strength of the past while growing and meeting the changing needs of its customers. When J.B. Atkinson organized local prominent citizens in 1919-1920 to look with real vision into the future, he created a solid and dependable institution within a growing and ever-changing community. Vancouver Federal Savings Bank remains an accurate reflection of the Vancouver community.

ALUMINUM COMPANY OF AMERICA VANCOUVER OPERATIONS

Alcoa manager C.S. Thayer describes potroom to President Franklin D. Roosevelt on a secret visit to Vancouver in 1942. Accompanying the President were his daughter, Anna, and his personal physician, Rear Admiral Ross McIntire, USN.

Aluminum Company of America's Vancouver Operations produced the first commercial aluminum west of the Mississippi River in 1940 as a response to President Franklin D. Roosevelt's call for new industrial customers to use surplus power generated by the newly constructed Northwest hydro dams. President Roosevelt, who made a secret visit to the plant after production began, believed that the aluminum industry could help pay for the Northwest's growing hydro system while bringing badly needed jobs into the Depression-battered region.

The following year the United States entered World War II, and the Vancouver Operations' objective changed to helping the nation gird for war in Europe and Asia. Throughout the war years manpower was at a premium. Portions of the plant had to be shut down periodically to keep the potrooms operational. Forty-eight-hour weeks were minimum with some employees working up to 118 hours per week. Production records reached an all-time high in January 1943, when enough aluminum was produced to manufacture 3,000 fighter planes or 1,600 bombers.

Plans for the West's first rod, wire, and cable mill were announced in 1947; however, it was not until two years later that construction actually began. The previous year the Columbia River had risen to its highest level in 50 years—more than 30 feet. Nine bulldozers worked around the clock to erect a dike. Offices were moved into Vancouver, and mill workers were transported by tugboat.

The rod, wire, and cable mill began production in 1950 and was expanded two years later, creating new jobs for 200 workers. Publicity for 1954 centered around a new $7-million extrusion mill, the first of its kind in the territory, and marked another step in the industry's progress in the Northwest.

A year later Alcoa unveiled its new corporate logo as employment at the Vancouver Operations topped 1,800.

In 1956 aluminum production capacity was expanded through potroom additions. The following year brought milestones for the plant—the rod mill rolled its one-millionth ingot, and the ingot department cast one million pounds of sheet ingot without a miscue. However, in 1958 production dropped by 60 percent due to a general business recession. Potline No. 4 was able to restart the following year, but production was again curtailed in 1962, this time due to Columbus Day's Hurricane Frieda. The storm caused heavy damage to the plant and forced a cutback. Restart of the fifth potline did not occur until 1963, when employment figures reached a five-year peak.

Two years later plans were announced for a Columbia River dock facility that would allow alumina to be unloaded directly from oceangoing vessels. The first shipment was received from Surinam, South America, with later ones arriving from Australia.

In 1965 Alcoa again set the pace in the Northwest by installing an insulated aluminum wire and cable manufacturing facility at Vancouver.

The first anodizing plant in the Alcoa system began operation in Vancouver in 1971. Three years later two pollution-control systems—the Alcoa 398 for potroom exhaust and the Alcoa 446 for carbon plant baking furnaces—were completed at a cost of $14 million. The 398 process is more than 98 percent efficient in keeping potential contaminants out of the atmosphere. At that point in the plant's history, employment had reached 1,544.

The year 1977 began with the disappointing shutdown of two potlines due to a curtailment of power supplied by the Bonneville Power Administration (BPA). However, the year was brightened by record production and the firm's announcement that $8.5 million had been approved for process and safety modernization projects. This represented the largest single expenditure for production facilities at Vancouver since the plant was constructed in 1940.

With electricity still of major concern and a regional power bill being considered by congress, the Vancouver Operations returned to full production in 1978. All personnel were recalled, and a new Alcoa CORE safety training program was initiated. For the first time in more than five years no hourly workers were laid off, and an additional 188 people were hired. However, 1979 again brought energy shortages as regional power demand outstripped supply. Two layoffs resulted as electric rates increased to pay for costly new nuclear power plants. These rate hikes changed aluminum's worldwide competitive position, and the future looked bleak for many plants, including Alcoa's Vancouver Operations.

At the close of 1980 President Jimmy Carter signed the long-awaited energy bill, almost three years after the first testimony was heard. The bill mandated that BPA offer new, long-term power contracts to its industrial customers, including Alcoa, and avoided an all-out battle over limited federal power resources. Despite the positive aspects of the bill, power costs for the plant soared from 7 to 26 mills, an increase of $75 million in two years. The plant dropped from five producing potlines to only two.

The challenges of poor economic conditions and increased power costs placed great demands on the plant. Employees more than met the test by forming a committee of 1,700 to work for more reasonable power costs. Cooperative Work Teams and Quality of Work Life Committees determined cost-saving projects and improved working relationships.

In the years that followed all areas of the plant felt the pressure of trying to compete in a world market. As a

In 1948 the Columbia River rose to over 30 feet, stranding the Vancouver Operations plant behind a dike built by employees.

result, it was necessary to make each production unit self-sufficient. Thus, in 1983 the extrusion plant spun off to form Vancouver Extrusion Company (Vanexco), a subsidiary of Alcoa. Historically, the plant had produced hard alloy extrusions for aerospace and agriculture. Today its markets are limited to soft alloy extrusions for residential and commercial windows and doors, truck-trailers, boat trailers, lighting fixtures, and shapes sold to metal distributors.

Two years later the rod, wire, and cable operation became a division of Alcoa Conductor Products Company (ACPC). This operation pioneered various shapes of conductor wire, including low-drag, wind-resistant electric transmission cable for utilities such as Bonneville. Its other products, including large, all-steel cable for crossing canyons and rivers, have worldwide markets.

Unfortunately, the smelter experienced its first total shutdown on June 3, 1986, when the Aluminum,

Brick, and Glass Workers International Union went on strike as a part of a national strike against Alcoa. A day later Alcoa officials announced that the shutdown would be permanent due to the expected costs to restart the facility. The action resulted in the loss of approximately 500 jobs at the plant; however, Alcoa Conductor Products Company and Vancouver Extrusion Company continued their operations.

Prior to the shutdown, smelting, extrusion, and cable annually added nearly $30 million to the community in wages, approximately $3 million in taxes, and more than $60 million in other goods and services purchased. Alcoans were involved in organizations throughout the area, and the Alcoa Foundation provided approximately $150,000 in grants to area educational institutions, the arts, and human service provider agencies.

While the future remains unclear for the aluminum industry in the Northwest, ACPC amd Vanexco employees continue to work hard at their jobs and in the community to be good corporate citizens and competitive firms in tomorrow's world market.

GREAT WESTERN MALTING CO.

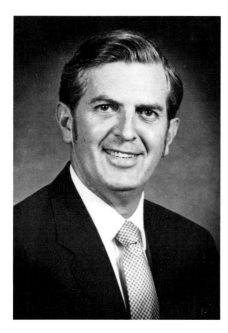

Ron Vogel, general manager.

---

*"This is the house that Jack built.
This is the malt
That lay in the house that Jack
built . . ."*

In Vancouver, a retired minister, a chemist, and a corporate president can trace the paths of their careers from the industry that inspired that nursery rhyme.

Prohibition ended in the United States in 1933. Two years later five men joined forces in Vancouver to establish Great Western Malting Co. Bill Einzig was the manager and organizer, Morgan Kellett was the operator. Emil Sick of Sick's Rainier Brewing, Seattle; Peter Schmidt of Olympia Brewing, Tumwater; and Arnold Blitz of Blitz-Weinhard, Portland, were the principal financiers.

A *Columbian* newspaper article dated July 18, 1935, described the new plant as "a never ceasing factory running 24 hours a day, 7 days a week." A total of 20 employees were supervised by Kellett.

It is hard to come up with a simple definition of malt. A maltster—what a malt maker calls himself—once ex-

plained malt as simply "barley with a frustrated life cycle." Transforming barley from the field into malt for the brewer is, however, both an art and a science. Malting barley is a specialty crop, painstakingly developed by experts skilled in plant genetics.

Great Western Malting Co. sought and acquired barleys of the highest brewing quality. The reason was pragmatic. Malt provides the principal source of beer flavor, the enzymes that start the brewing process, and is the main material from which beer is made.

Orme Kellett went to work for his father as a part-time laborer the year the plant began operation. A bright student, he received a master's degree in chemistry and biology from the University of Wisconsin.

Morgan Kellett was killed in an automobile accident in 1946. Following his death, Orme Kellett became vice-president of production at the Great Western plant. He was with Great Western until 1973, when he went to Oxford, England, finishing studies to be ordained as a full-time Episcopal priest.

Malting a grain is simply to sprout it under controlled temperatures. It is germinated, then dried or roasted.

In Europe, the first malt houses

Located near the site of the old World War I shipyards on Port of Vancouver property, Great Western Malting Co. dwells in a canyon of grain elevators.

were floor malt houses. Workers with wooden shovels turned the barley and spread it out on the floor to aerate it. Stored grain can heat up, so Great Western continued to develop increasingly efficient methods to improve the process. The present system places the barley in large beds with helixes that stir it and keep it loose. The floor is perforated, and large fans cool it from underneath.

In 1964 the management of Great Western reorganized and bought the company from the brewers. They were independent until 1969, when they organized a conglomerate called Columbia Corporation, headquartered in Portland, Oregon. Two principals were Cal Souther, a prominent Portland attorney who resided in Ridgefield, and Russell Hamachek, president of Great Western Malting Co. and later of Columbia Corporation. Columbia Corporation was dissolved and sold to UNIVAR, based in Seattle.

Tod Hamachek took the helm of Great Western Malting Co. when his father retired. At the age of 31, with a master's degree in business administration from Harvard, he had previously served as a national marketing manager for a firm that sold large commercial offset printing presses. He joined Great Western in 1974 in sales and marketing. Elevated to vice-president of sales in 1977, he became president of the firm at the end of that year.

In a 1980 interview Hamachek noted that he had inherited the best management group in the malting business. "I'm not a maltster and I'm not a chemist. I need a lot of these people more than they need me."

His management team included corporate executives who were well respected in the Vancouver community. Charles Coatney, vice-president of finance, had joined Great Western in 1957. He served as president and chairman of the board of the Greater Vancouver Chamber of Commerce in 1982 and 1983. Coatney passed away in 1985, following a courageous bout with cancer.

Quentin Stoda, the company's current vice-president/finance, served on the Vancouver School Board and the original board of Southwest Washington Independent Forward Thrust (SWIFT), a charitable community fund-raising group that was formed in 1977.

Charles Unger was with Great Western from 1955 until 1986. A chamber of commerce president in 1968, he managed the Los Angeles plant until his retirement.

At the end of 1982 Great Western launched its new cogeneration power plant. A natural-gas-powered turbine engine, with the same basic design as the one that powers a DC-10 airplane, produces enough electricity to light and heat 8,000 homes. The electricity is sold to the Clark County Public Utility District, and the heat generated is used by Great Western in its process.

In 1984 the firm, previously under UNIVAR, became a division of Penwest, Ltd. There are now two manufacturing companies: Great Western Malting, and Penick and Ford, a corn wet-milling facility in Iowa. Hamachek heads Penwest, and Ron Vogel serves as executive vice-president and general manager of Great Western Malting with plants in Vancouver, Los Angeles, and Pocatello, Idaho.

A maltster on top of a rail car loads a steady stream of malt. Maltsters and master brewers are accorded the same professionsal status in the beer-making industry.

A native of Vancouver, Vogel was born at the old St. Joseph Hospital. He graduated from the original Vancouver High School and attended the University of Washington. After earning a bachelor's degree in chem-

Temperature control has reached an exact science with this high-technology control room.

istry, he joined Great Western Malting as a laboratory technician. Five years later he became corporate quality control manager for the company. By 1979 he was vice-president of sales, and five years later he took over as general manager.

Vogel's father worked at Fort Vancouver Plywood, located next to Great Western's plant. When the young chemist joined Great Western, he packed a sack lunch each day and walked over to his father's saw-filing shop to chat during his lunch hour. The elder Vogel had been active in the Depression years, organizing a union at the plywood plant. He and eight others were fired because of their activities, but eventually were rehired, and he worked 40 years at the plant next to Great Western.

For 20 years Great Western has shipped malt into the export market. By year-end 1984 the firm had exported a record quantity of malt to the Orient and also was shipping to the Philippines. Then the strong U.S. dollar and subsidized competitors from Europe, Canada, and Australia forced Great Western out of the Pacific Rim market.

Under Vogel's leadership Great Western Malting Co. began to reach out to new domestic markets. Sales of high-quality barley malt have traditionally been strong in the West. However, the continued consolidation of national breweries and the government subsidies that benefit its international competitors have resulted in Great Western's marketing thrust into new areas within the United States, such as Virginia, Missouri, Texas, Florida, and North Carolina.

Great Western Malting Co. is held in esteem by brewers worldwide. The firm is consistently rated among the top four malting companies from 17 countries. Annual malt sales top $75 million, and its employees number approximately 250.

HEWLETT PACKARD COMPANY

In the summer of 1979 five people arrived at Portland International Airport each Friday to meet and plan what was to become a Hewlett Packard plant that would employ 510 workers in 1986. Jim Doub, general manager of the new facility, and Ardis Zidan, director of human resources, flew each week from the HP plant in Cupertino, California. Joe Conrad, manufacturing, and Bob Foco, controller, came from Fort Collins, Colorado. Nilesh Gheewala, head of research and development, made his Friday voyage from San Diego.

The new venture was a spin-off from three other areas. It consolidated the research and development of products being manufactured at that time in Boise, Fort Collins, and Cupertino. The goal was to start a printer division in Vancouver. The printers were designed to be used with Hewlett Packard computer systems and terminals.

The five-member group met at the Red Lion Inn at Jantzen Beach every week to recruit professional engineers and their families to join the Vancouver operation and build a permanent staff. At a wine and cheese reception, local realtors presented a slide show and the team told the Hewlett Packard story—an unusual tale indeed.

In 1938 Bill Hewlett and Dave Packard, close friends and engineering graduates of Stanford University, set up shop in a one-car garage behind the Packard's rented home in Palo Alto, California. There the two men developed what was to be the first product of their lifelong partnership.

The product was a new type of audio oscillator—an electronic instrument used to test sound equipment. Hewlett had designed the circuitry as a thesis subject at Stanford while working toward his engineering degree. Later that year the partners pre-

Hewlett Packard's present 175,000-square-foot building in East Vancouver.

sented the product at a West Coast meeting of the Institute of Radio Engineers. They called it the Model 200A "because the number sounded bigger."

The presentation landed them a few orders and their first important contract with Walt Disney Studios, which needed an oscillator having a different physical configuration to develop the unique sound system for the classic film, *Fantasia.* With that first big order on the books, Hewlett and Packard formally organized their partnership in 1939.

During World War II Hewlett served in the Army and Packard kept the business going. Production was constant, new measuring instruments were designed, and by 1946 HP had moved into the microwave measuring field. By 1950 the firm had 200 employees, 70 products, and two million dollars in sales. In 1956 a new manufacturing complex and corporate

headquarters was built in Stanford Industrial Park. Two years later the product line included 373 electronic test and measuring instruments and accessories. Customers at the time were scientists and engineers.

Hewlett Packard introduced its first computer in 1966 to gather and analyze the data produced by its electronic instruments. By 1985 computers, computer systems, terminals, printers, plotters, disk and tape drives, and calculators accounted for more than half of the company's sales revenue of $6.51 billion. Today the firm employs nearly 84,000 people, 56,000 of whom work in the United States. Other research and manufacturing facilities are located in Europe, Japan, Latin America, Canada, and Southeast Asia. Sales and support offices cover the globe.

From the beginning employee benefits and employee involvement were major concerns at Hewlett Packard. The "HP Way" is built on teamwork, consensus, communication, and individual worth. One element of the company's style has been

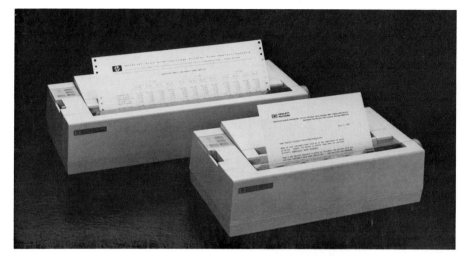

HP Vancouver's most recent entry into the printer market is the Quietjet Printer Series.

described as "management by walking around."

That style is the same wherever Hewlett Packard has a facility. Ardis Zidan recalls the five-member team's Friday evening sessions with warm memories. The first "office" was set up in a leased temporary location on Northeast 65th Avenue near Fort Vancouver High School. Employees entered through "roll-up" metal doors. There were five small black rented desks, one black phone, one receptionist, and one bathroom. The first model printer was called the 9871, and Zidan describes it as "efficient, but ugly." The first product shipment occurred on October 31, 1979, and the pioneer team of employees celebrated with a big Halloween party.

In 1979 Hewlett Packard purchased 192 acres in Cascade Park on Southeast 34th Street from GenStar. Because of stiff competition in the printer market and economic downturns in the computer industry, the company did not effect the move into the $15-million facility it built there until 1982.

At that time the high-tech firm converted 75 percent of its production operation to a stockless production concept modeled after what the Japanese called Kanban, and applied it to all printers manufactured at the

The Vancouver Division's first revenue-producing product, the 9871 Daisy Wheel Impact Printer.

site. Presently 100 percent of the firm's products use this method, and the Vancouver Division is a recognized leader in the development of this manufacturing technology and hosts hundreds of visitors each year from other HP manufacturing sites and companies throughout the world to learn about this technique.

Stockless production has changed the nature of the job from one of a need for single-task dexterity to multiple-task assignment and participative productivity enhancements.

The firm's Vancouver plant has expanded its capacity and design capability to include the production of printers for most types of personal computers and work stations, including IBM, Hewlett Packard, Apple,

and other major manufacturers. The HP niche in the market is "quiet printers." Impact printing was the first technology produced at Vancouver. Thermal technology was subsequently developed to provide solutions in a different market segment. That developed into the newest development of the Vancouver product designers and producers is Ink Jet printers that rapidly "spit" ink on the paper for better production quality and quieter operation.

In 1984 Hewlett Packard moved again to consolidate products. The Corvallis, Oregon, unit developing the Ink Jet technology moved 35 people into the research and development division of the Vancouver plant, though the actual product is made in Singapore. All of the support for the product is done at Vancouver. The printer division of HP in Vancouver holds a significant position in the international market.

Bob Watson, general manager of the Vancouver Hewlett Packard facility, came to the area in 1985 from the Boise operation where he spent four years as research and development manager for six HP information systems including the Vancouver operation. In keeping with the HP Way, Watson's office is in an open corner. A space with no doors, it is sectioned off only by modular dividers.

Watson believes there is a revolution going on in the electronics industry and that the survivors must change their goals and become focused more on research to meet customer's needs rapidly and increase marketing expertise.

Since 1980 production volume at the Hewlett Packard Company's Vancouver plant has more than doubled. In 1986 the facility employed 510 people.

COLUMBIA MACHINE, INC.

In 1937 Fred Neth, Sr., began what was to be a worldwide corporation in this small building at the corner of Fifth and Main streets.

In 1937 Fred Neth started a small family business in a one-story building at the corner of Fifth and Main streets in downtown Vancouver. A simple sign read: "Columbia Machine Works, Acetylene—Electric Welding—Structural Steel—Blacksmithing." Today, nearly 50 years later, Columbia Machine, Inc., is a multimillion-dollar worldwide manufacturing corporation. The company is currently one of the world's largest suppliers for the concrete block-manufacturing industry and for palletizing operations in a wide range of industries. Fred Neth, Sr., serves as chairman of the board of Columbia Machine; his son Tom Neth is president and chief executive officer; and Fred Neth, Jr., manages operations.

In the late 1940s Fred Sr. was repairing a machine that had been brought to his shop. The natural engineering genius that was to lead him to eventual global prominence resulted in a design he conceived and built—a hydraulically operated, fully automatic concrete block-making machine that was far more advanced than others being manufactured at the time. By the early 1950s the name "Columbia" was well known throughout the United States and Canada, and its line of machinery had expanded to include larger, more sophisticated production equipment.

Columbia's headquarters on Southeast Grand is built of concrete blocks produced by its own machines. Even the paving stones of the sidewalk were produced by the firm's equipment.

Columbia is the only firm in the world that offers complete, fully automated manufacturing plants, including turnkey operations that perform all plant functions from raw aggregate and cement batching to the cured blocks delivered to the storage yard—all with state-of-the-art total automation.

The company's headquarters was built at its present location, 107 Grand Boulevard, in the late 1940s. Directly across the state highway was the booming Kaiser Shipyard operation. During World War II Columbia contracted with the shipyard for numerous machine work jobs. After the war the temporary housing that had filled the adjacent area was torn down, and Columbia expanded its plant to the site of the movie theater originally used by shipyard workers.

By the late 1950s Columbia Machine dominated the U.S. domestic market and had increased its manufacturing facilities in order to enter the export market. By the 1980s the firm was doing business in more than 70 countries, with offices in Japan, Australia, New Zealand, and Mexico. Sales and service representatives are based in other areas, and licensed manufacturers operate in Japan and Australia.

Paradoxically, the industry in

130

which Columbia Machine is the major innovator serves climates and areas much different than those of the northwestern United States. Timber is used in the Northwest for homes and many major structures, while in Arizona, Nevada, Southern California, Florida, and Hawaii virtually every structure is of concrete blocks. In those climates timber is scarce or often does not remain stable.

High-quality, exposed, load-bearing blocks are becoming increasingly popular throughout the world. As a result, Columbia Machine has placed a priority on expansion to meet the growing demand for its machinery. There are two manufacturing facilities in North America—Vancouver, Washington, and Toronto, Canada. There are parts depots in Ontario, Canada, and Orlando, Florida, and a warehouse in Mattoon, Illinois. A subsidiary operates in Australia, and a sales office and parts center is located in New Zealand.

The firm's line of production machinery includes block machines in 22 basic models—from a portable one-block machine to a pacesetting 20-ton six-block production giant. A single machine can turn out thousands of varieties of blocks. Columbia Machine takes pride in its intensive engineering research and development staff that studies market needs and continuously produces new designs to meet the needs of a thriving industry. Because it offers machines that cover the spectrum, from simple to state of the art, the company is able to serve third world developing countries as well as highly industrialized heavily populated nations. Equipment combinations can be engineered specifically to a customer's individual production requirements.

As Tom Neth points out, "Our equipment uses hydraulics rather than the gear-driven machinery produced by a major competitor. This gives us a further advantage. Because

Columbia's model 60, a six-block-at-a-time machine, is setting the standard for high-quality and dependable production.

we still offer a one- or two-block machine, we can work with a newly developing country at the onset and offer an upgrade when the time is necessary." A machine purchased by a firm in the Netherlands is the largest producer to date, turning out 500 2-inch by 3.875-inch by 8.25-inch bricks per minute.

In the early 1960s Columbia Machine adapted a concrete block-cubing machine to create a palletizer for the general materials-handling industry. Eagerly accepted in the marketplace, the invention led to the formation of a new division, Materials Handling. The company then expanded the palletizer product line to include floor-level machines for the bottling and food industries. Those machines were followed by others designed to stack pails and bags. By the early 1980s that division had developed the most complete line of palletizers available

in North America, and had earned a reputation as the "Cadillac" of the industry. The machines, which are sold to virtually all consumer-oriented industries, are fully automated and programmable, enabling product flow to be efficiently accomplished according to each customer's unique product specifications.

Instruction and training programs for clients worldwide are offered several times a year through specialized schools at the firm's Vancouver headquarters. More recently Columbia Machine has shipped two complete block-making plants to the People's Republic of China. With the aid of skilled interpreters, Chinese production leaders were among those trained at the Vancouver plant.

According to Tom Neth, teamwork has been a major factor in the firm's dynamic growth and position of worldwide leadership. "Our objective," he says, "is to maintain that sense of teamwork in an atmosphere of open communication and respect for the individual people who together are Columbia Machine, Inc."

LANDERHOLM, MEMOVICH, LANSVERK AND WHITESIDES, INC., P.S.

"We have chosen Vancouver. Our homes, our families, and our hearts are here. Our roots are deep in this land of the river, the mountains, the tall firs, roses, and rhododendrons. We have chosen the law—to serve Vancouver through this honorable profession."

A permanent investment in the community of Vancouver as a place to exercise one's professional life is a commitment that the largest law firm in Southwest Washington asks of its partners and staff when they join. The firm opened its doors to clients 38 years ago in the old Ford Building at Sixth and Main streets in Vancouver. Landerholm, Memovich, Lansverk and Whitesides, Inc., P.S., moved to its present location at 915 Broadway in the Pacific First Federal Savings Bank Building in 1975 and has expanded its office there to accommodate the needs of the growing Clark County and Southwest Washington population.

Landerholm, Memovich, Lansverk and Whitesides strives to be a full-service law firm. The firm handles both civil and criminal litigation,

with a goal of excellence in service to its clients. Special consideration is given to hiring qualified attorneys to practice in key areas of service to the community. The members of the firm have contributed a total of 183 years of service to the community in various areas of practice. In addition to providing general legal services to the community, the firm emphasizes practice in the areas of taxation, land use, business planning, estate planning, personal injury litigation, worker's compensation, and social security entitlements. Members of the firm are active in various organizations related to the practice of law. Among the firm's attorneys are three former presidents and three former treasurers of the Clark County Bar Association, and current or former members of various committees and the board of governors of the Washington State Bar Association and Washington State Trial Lawyers' Association.

In addition to serving on professional committees, the members of the firm are active in the community, helping to direct numerous service organizations including the Vancou-

Members of the Landerholm law firm (seated, from left): Dale V. Whitesides, Duane Lansverk, Richard T. Howsley, Irwin C. Landerholm, Kevin G. Staples, and Steven A. Memovich. In the back row (from left): Jackson H. Welch, Gregory J. Dennis, Kay J. Leffel, Larry O. Klossner, Marla R. Ludolph, William H. Reed, William C. Dudley, Elizabeth A. Perry, and Robert J. Harris. Absent: T. Randall Grove.

ver School District, Vancouver Kiwanis, Southwest Washington Hospitals, Clark County Civil Service Commission, Clark College Foundation, Southwest Washington Hospital Foundation, Clark County Community Foundation, Catholic Community Services, and various church boards and committees.

The active involvement of its members reflects the concern of Landerholm, Memovich, Lansverk and Whitesides, Inc., P.S., for the community. The members of the firm have chosen the law, chosen Vancouver, and have chosen to serve their community well—in the past, and continuing in the future.

VERNON F. PETERSON & ASSOCIATES, P.S.

The senior partner of one of Vancouver's oldest and most stable accounting partnerships joined the accounting profession almost by accident. That's half of the story of Vernon F. Peterson & Associates, P.S. Today the firm employs a total of seven CPAs in two cities. That growth is the other half of the story.

In 1958 Vernon Peterson was still planning to be an attorney. He was finishing his first year of law school at Willamette School of Law in Salem. But, having a degree in business administration from Walla Walla College, when he needed employment he found a job with Mickelwait and Brown (now Moss Adams), a Vancouver accounting firm. The position, located via the classified ads, started a distinguished accounting career.

Over the years Peterson has returned to the community much time and assistance. He has been an officer in a Kiwanis Club, president of the Greater Vancouver Chamber of Commerce, treasurer of the Salvation Army, and chairman of the Columbia River Development Association. He has also served the accounting profession on committees at both the state and national levels.

Peterson set up his own office in 1962 in Hazel Dell at 7702 Northeast Fifth Avenue. He had no employees, and all the office work was done by his wife, Jelene, on an as-needed basis. Five years later the firm had two employees, and moved to a larger space at 7601 Northeast Hazel Dell Avenue. In January 1976 the company settled at its present location, 7917 Northeast Hazel Dell Avenue, in a building owned by and especially constructed for Vernon F. Peterson & Associates, P.S.

Peterson began adding associates in 1968 when Ron Oliver arrived from California. Like Peterson, Oliver was headed for another career. One year of medical school convinced him

The professional staff consists of (left to right) Newton Rumble, Dennis Hatton, Patricia Eby, Ronald Oliver, and Vernon Peterson. Russ Tyner was not present. Photo by David Simmons

that his first choice was not right for him. After leaving medical school in 1967, he worked in a Kaiser steel mill in Fontana, California, and took a correspondence course in accounting. He then wrote to Peterson, whom he did not know, asking for work. Peterson responded that he had enough work to keep him from January 1 through April 15. They have been partners since 1970. Although Oliver never took an accounting class in college, he later took classes at Portland State University, received an M.B.A., and is also a certified management accountant.

In 1970 Peterson incorporated his practice into Vernon F. Peterson & Associates, P.S. He now has three co-owners: Ron Oliver, Duane Gilliland, and Dennis Hatton. Another of the CPAs in the firm, Patsy Eby, is also an attorney.

Gilliland is also a graduate of Walla Walla College and holds a degree in business administration. He

joined the firm in September 1974 as a result of Peterson's request of his alma mater to alert him to good graduates. In August 1982 Gilliland moved to Mount Vernon to open a branch office that was created when the company bought out an existing practice. Hatton came from Oliver's alma mater, Pacific Union College, in 1979. He manages the firm's extensive computer operations.

The company has merged with a number of other accounting firms in the Vancouver area. Harriet Sandstrom of Battle Ground was the first, in 1968. More recent mergers were with Hal Smith and Russ Tyner. Tyner is presently a member of the staff.

The work of CPAs has changed considerably, since the firm was founded. The focus, in those days, was on private companies and income tax returns. Today the emphasis is on complete financial planning services. To assure that Vernon F. Peterson & Associates, P.S., continually serves its clients in the best way possible, Peterson is especially proud that the firm belongs to the Private Companies Practice Section of the AICPA (American Institute of CPAs). That means that every three years the company undergoes a peer review by another CPA firm.

SEH AMERICA, INC.

Since 1980 Vancouver has been the U.S. headquarters for SEH America, Inc. The firm is a subsidiary of Shin-Etsu Handotai Company, Ltd., the world's leading supplier of silicon and epitaxial wafers, with plant operations in Japan, Malaysia, the United Kingdom, and the United States. A semiconductor materials company, SEH America supplies the flat, round, meticulously finished silicon wafers on which chip makers pattern electronic circuits used in consumer, automotive, industrial, data-processing, and military applications.

Wafer production begins with polycrystalline silicon, the raw material from which SEH grows high-purity, single-crystal silicon ingots. Produced in sizes up to eight inches in diameter, the ingots are sliced into wafers, polished, and, for certain applications, given an epitaxial (epi) layer.

Wafer dimensions are exact. SEH must produce virtual "zero-defect" yields for its customers. Therefore, quality work is essential, and production takes place in work areas that are as much as 50,000 times more clean than the average operating room.

At SEH quality is more than a production standard. It is an attitude that starts with every person, every sales order, every step of the production process. That quality is reflected in the total work environment. The

Completed in June 1984, SEH America's U.S. corporate headquarters for both administration and manufacturing is located at 4111 Northeast 112th Avenue.

firm's commitment to quality, therefore, is to employees, to customers, and to area residents and the environment in which SEH operates.

The company's multimillion-dollar investment in environmental control and safety at the Vancouver operation is viewed by management as an integral part of the cost of doing business. The complex is widely recognized by the Washington State Department of Ecology, other government agencies, and the semiconductor industry as a well-designed facility. The Pacific Northwest Pollution Control Association presented SEH America with a Washington State Award for the design, installa-

tion, and operation of its innovative chemical waste-treatment and pollution-abatement system.

The firm's total investment in its U.S. headquarters complex is about $80 million. SEH began production in a temporary facility in Vancouver in 1980. The silicon wafer plant, the first SEH production facility built in the United States, was dedicated on September 11, 1984. The 61-acre site features a 175,000-square-foot silicon ingot and wafer plant and a 60,000-square-foot epitaxial wafer plant. Both are state-of-the-art manufacturing facilities.

SEH employs approximately 750 people at its U.S. facility, and 90 percent of the work force lives in Clark County. The corporation was attracted to Vancouver, in large part, by the friendliness of the community. Since its arrival, the company has demonstrated that its investment is not in facilities alone, but also in the community.

SEH America, Inc., played a significant role in the establishment of the Southwest Washington Joint Center for Education and has actively assisted business and community leaders in attracting other high-tech firms to Clark County.

In April 1985 a second major building was completed on the 61-acre site. Shown (lower left) is the building that houses the epitaxial wafer facility.

THE VANCOUVER CLINIC

In July 1929, a time when office calls were $2 and house calls $2.50, Dr. John C. Brougher began his practice with Dr. C.R. Zener in a newly constructed Medical Arts Building. Upon Dr. Zener's retirement in 1930, Dr. Brougher assumed responsibility for the organization that was to eventually become The Vancouver Clinic. In May 1939 Dr. Brougher joined with three other physicians—Frank Boersma, H. Leslie Frewing, and David Loree—to form the Vancouver Medical and Surgical Clinic. The facility would provide Clark County with multiple specialties under one roof, a tradition that would continue through the years. Known since 1941 as The Vancouver Clinic, the once-small group has become Clark County's largest medical clinic.

The Vancouver Clinic remained in

the Medical Arts Building until the mid-1950s, when expansion within the structure could no longer continue. On June 15, 1956, a new facility at 111 West 39th Street was opened. Vancouver and the surrounding area continued to grow during the next two decades, increasing the need for additional highly trained medical specialists. The Vancouver Clinic met that need through selective additions of critically needed specialists and subspecialists. By the mid-1970s, however, the 39th Street location could no longer accommodate the increased number of patients and staff.

In 1977 ground was broken at 700 Northeast 87th Avenue for the clinic's new offices. The 38,000-square-foot, $2.5-million project was completed three months ahead of schedule and today serves as The Vancouver Clinic's main office. When Dr. Brougher retired in 1979 after 50

Left:
The Vancouver Medical Clinic was housed in the Medical Arts Building from 1936 until 1956.

Below:
From 1956 to 1979 the Vancouver Clinic operated in this facility on 111 West 39th Street.

Bottom:
The current location of the Vancouver Clinic, at 700 Northeast 87th Avenue.

years of medical practice, the facility employed 20 physicians in its four specialties—obstetrics/gynecology, internal medicine, pediatrics, and general surgery. The clinic continued its growth, and in 1986 two family practitioners were added, bringing the total number of physicians to 34 within 5 specialties. The Vancouver Clinic employs a full-time staff of 112.

Medicine has changed over the years, and the new trend is toward more individualized care. In 1986 The Vancouver Clinic opened two satellite offices: one in Battle Ground and the other in Camas. These offices were designed to be closer to the residences of a large number of the institution's patients.

The Vancouver Clinic has plans for the future that include expansion within its existing specialties as the population of the area continues to grow. The facility expects to make changes in the delivery of services as the nature of medicine changes. This flexible approach results from years of experience in responding to the ever-changing needs of its patients.

One notable example of this change is the fact that today a substantial number of people do not have a family doctor, relying instead on hospital emergency rooms and urgency care clinics. When The Vancouver Clinic's new offices were built, a special urgency care clinic was added to take care of those people who did not yet have a family doctor or required immediate attention at times when their own physician was unavailable.

The physicians and staff members currently associated with The Vancouver Clinic, as well as those who have retired, have been active in the civic affairs of the Vancouver/Clark County community. Over the years they have been participating members in local service clubs, advisory boards, and in community efforts to improve local health care delivery.

VANCOUVER FURNITURE

In the middle of World War II a Eugene, Oregon, couple, Joseph G. and Goldie Weinstein, sold their successful men's clothing business and opened two furniture stores in Vancouver in 1946. Their oldest son, Allan, returned from 34 months in the Pacific with the United States Army, spent a short time in Eugene, then moved to Vancouver to learn the furniture business from Si Cohn, the manager.

At that time Vancouver Furniture had five full-time employees: Milt Carl, now a Portland realtor; Cohn; Ann Martin; Fred Hughes; and Allan Weinstein. Two delivery men also worked part time at the 11th and Washington streets location, which had been an automobile repair garage. Volume the first year was $180,000. By 1953 the volume topped $400,000, and Joseph Weinstein chose to build at a new location, the present site of Vancouver Furniture at 11th and Broadway. Tom Adams had the structure built, and the facility is still known as the Adams Building. Allan and Melvin Weinstein eventually purchased it.

When the Van Port flood of 1948 washed out the highway in the Oregon Delta Park area, Allan Weinstein was still living in Portland. Each day he made his way to Vancouver, despite the odds. One day he traveled by seaplane. The pilot, who wore waders, landed in the water near Pearson Air Park, and had Weinstein, in suit and tie, hop on his back to be "piggybacked" to shore where he called a taxi.

Melvin Weinstein, Allan's younger brother, joined Vancouver Furniture in 1954. That year the brothers bought out their father's interest in the firm. Melvin, who had been part of an Army efficiency team during the Korean Conflict, took over the firm's financial and credit responsibilities. Allan supervised merchandising and sales promotion. By 1956 the

Melvin Weinstein

company had 25 employees. They entered a contest sponsored by the National Brand Names Foundation and won the "Oscar" of the national home furnishings industry, Brand Name Retailer of the Year—Furniture Division. The award was presented to them in New York City at the Waldorf Astoria in 1957; the evening's entertainment was Steve Allen's original "Tonight Show."

Allan Weinstein

By 1971 yearly volume had grown to $1.25 million and seven years later it reached the $3-million mark, with 40 employees. Both men had involved themselves for years in the community and the Business and Professional Committee of the Greater Vancouver Chamber of Commerce. Melvin has served on the Southwest Washington Hospitals Board and the Columbian Advisory Board, and is a member of the Vancouver Planning Commission. Allan has served on Community First Federal Savings Board, was a founder of the SWIFT Auction, and is a trustee of Evergreen State College.

The firm is active in the local Stop Hunger program and has been contributing trade-in furniture to destitute families since 1981. It participates in programs to help supply the local food banks on a regular basis.

In 1978 Vancouver Furniture built a new 30,000-square-foot warehouse/ showroom at 7017 Northeast St. Johns Road. The following year it installed a $100,000 computer system to keep track of mushrooming sales, inventory control, and accounts receivable.

A more serious marketing thrust began in 1982. With Portland competitors actively trying to attract southwest Washington consumers, the partners decided to compete aggressively. Projected volume for 1986 is expected to triple that of 1978. An additional warehouse space of 17,000 square feet was purchased early in 1986. The computer capacity has been doubled, and the firm now has six delivery trucks and 78 employees, including a sales force of 25 people. Nearly 30 percent of the yearly volume comes from 83 communities in Oregon. Characteristically modest, Allan and Melvin Weinstein attribute Vancouver Furniture's growth to "a strong middle-management team of five professionals: two women and three men."

144

VANCOUVER MALL

Billed as the first two-level, climate-controlled, enclosed shopping center in the Northwest, Vancouver Mall officially opened its doors in August 1977. The $50-million complex took nearly two years to construct. The general contractors were Emerick Construction, Portland; S.D. Spencer and Sons, Vancouver; and Overbay Construction, Vancouver. The shopping center is located on 97.2 acres in the industrial and commercial growth corridor of Clark County.

Bob Scheetz, original owner of the property, saw an article in *Fortune* magazine concerning the top shopping center developers in the United States. Scheetz had a dream to have a regional shopping center built on property he wished to sell. He placed several phone calls to the heads of the development firms listed in the magazine. May Centers, Inc., of St. Louis, Missouri, purchased the land, and seven years later, in August 1977, Phase I of Vancouver Mall was opened.

Phase I consisted of Meier & Frank, Sears, Nordstrom, and specialty stores totaling 660,000 square feet. The second phase, which officially opened in 1980, added JCPenney, Mervyn's, and specialty stores with a square footage of 438,000. The entire mall area now encompasses more than one million square feet.

Located on 97.2 acres near the intersection of SR 500 and Interstate 205, Vancouver Mall was built on land once used for small farms.

With more than 120 stores, including five major department stores and a bank, Vancouver Mall provides a relaxed shopping environment for area residents.

With more than 120 stores, including five major department stores, specialty stores, and a bank, Vancouver Mall is varied and comprehensive in the range of goods and services offered to its customers. The facility also offers a variety of community services, including a community room for meetings, a public library, and a Customer Service Center, which contains a Department of Licensing subagency, voter registration, and other services available to customers.

Although merchandising is the primary purpose of Vancouver Mall, creating a sense of identity with the community and local residents is an important aspect of its operation. Community ties are so strong that citizens feel possessive about the center and participate often in the varied activities that occur there. Major community fairs, displays, and exhibitions are regularly scheduled every month by the mall's marketing department with the active participation of the merchants. Events such as Health and Book fairs, Community Awareness days, and Art fairs put on by local elementary and secondary schools are regular events at Vancouver Mall.

The steady patronage of old as well as new customers who return time and again to renew their acquaintance with the facility has made Vancouver Mall a successful shopping center.

145

HIDDEN BRICK COMPANY

Foster Hidden, son of the founder, casing up a kiln in 1928.

When George Washington made brick in the 1700s he did it the same way that the Hidden Brick Company has been manufacturing its brick since 1871. Hidden makes the only sandmold brick west of the Mississippi River. All other manufacturers have abandoned the labor-intensive, and therefore significantly more expensive, sandmold process for an extrusion process. In the sandmold process, clay is mixed with water and then placed in a wooden mold that has been soaked in water and dusted with dry sand. The sand acts like flour in a cake pan, allowing the newly formed brick to be dumped out of the mold. The "green" brick is then air dried for about a week and baked in the kiln for another week.

Soon after his arrival in Vancouver in 1864, Lowell M. Hidden, a native of Vermont, helped a gentleman named Mr. Armstrong construct a brewery building at Sixth and Columbia. Hidden's job was to carry the brick and mortar and generally help with the construction. Armstrong had made the brick from plentiful clay deposits he had found in Vancouver.

Hidden held other jobs over the next few years, one of which was hewing timbers for the piling at the dock with a Mr. Ginder, who was also from Vermont. They were paid for the job in gold, which they converted into paper money three to one. Both men then purchased 400 acres near Cherry Grove (92nd Avenue and 219th Street) for the equivalent of about one dollar an acre.

In 1871 Mother Joseph approached Hidden and asked him to make the brick for the academy she planned to build. Armstrong had left town, but Hidden knew how to make brick. He teamed up with Ginder and established a brickyard at 15th and Main where one end of the clay deposit was located. The clay ran from that point in a northwesterly direction to the present location of the brickyard at 27th and Kauffman. The deposit was just below the topsoil and reached a depth of approximately six feet.

By the 1920s Hidden Brothers was making 20,000 brick per day using 45 yards of clay. Every two or three months they fired 300,000 brick at one time. This process used 100 cords of wood, mostly from the nearby slab mills, but also from the Cherry Grove acreage. Smoke filled the air during the one week it took to burn the brick.

In 1929 Mayor Kiggins ran on a platform to extend Washington Street through the brickyard. The yard extended from Main Street west to 54 feet west of Washington Street between 14th and 16th streets. By then the yard was operated by Hidden's sons, Foster and Oliver. Mayor Kiggins was elected, the city

Malcom Ruiter, Fred Prew, Bob Dobmire, unknown, Mr. Stewart, Mr. Schweigert, Bill Walters, Frank Nickerson, Al Thompson, Andrew Thompson, unknown, Foster Hidden, and Oliver Hidden (from left) at Hidden Brothers Brick Yard in 1910. The old Congregational Church, also built in 1910, is barely visible in the background above the brickyard smoke. (Inset) The Hidden Brothers brickyard circa 1945.

bought the right of way, Oliver retired from the business, and Foster moved the yard to its present location, taking his son Robert into the business with him. That same year a date was put on some of the brick for the first time; the Hidden name had been imprinted since 1905.

Prior to moving the yard, the deposit of clay was being used up. Hidden owned 25 lots at 19th and Daniels and had begun digging clay there 20 years before the yard was moved. Hough School was built on the site because there were no houses that needed to be torn down and the excavation had been done. The school brought in $800 worth of dirt to build up the playing field when the project was complete.

Robert Hidden still makes sandmold brick almost the same way his grandfather Lowell did. He now has machinery to help the process, but the product is the same. Lowell Hidden sold his brick for seven dollars per thousand; they currently sell for 60 cents apiece.

Many of Vancouver's buildings were constructed of Hidden brick. The Providence Academy was the largest brick building north of San Francisco when it was completed in 1873. From 1960 to 1983 the firm supplied all the material for the C.F. Braun Company buildings in California. At present the brick is used for historical restorations, such as the Jewish synagogue in Victoria, British Columbia. Hidden Brick Company's last major construction project was a seven-story building—all brick—in Alhambra, California.

THE COLUMBIAN

On October 10, 1890, the first issue of *The Columbian* was published in a second-floor office at 215 Main Street. The four-page weekly was a staunch supporter of the Democrats and was often embroiled in political feuds with its Republican rival, *The Independent.*

The four pages grew to eight in 1900, and under new management, the newspaper turned its support to the Republicans. Page size and format changed frequently, even after *The Columbian* began daily publication in 1908. Political affiliations were also uncertain as the company underwent a series of ownership changes. Stability was finally achieved when the newspaper was purchased by Herbert Campbell in 1921, and firmly established as a political independent.

Campbell, a well-known Northwest newspaperman, moved the plant to a renovated post office building at Fourth and Washington, but rapid growth soon forced him to have a new facility constructed at Tenth and Broadway. That site remained the home of *The Columbian* until it was moved to its present location at Eighth and Grant in 1955.

Though circulation was up and down during the Depression years of the 1930s, *The Columbian* survived.

The Columbian *began publishing daily in 1908. This picture of the second-floor office at 215 Main Street is believed to have been taken around 1910.*

Soon after purchasing the newspaper in 1921, Herbert Campbell had this building constructed on the corner of Tenth and Broadway. The Columbian *remained at this site until 1955.*

Other area newspapers that attempted to publish daily were not successful. *The Sun,* a weekly for 39 years, failed three years after beginning daily publication. *The Columbian* bought its circulation list and for a time was published as *The Vancouver Columbian and The Sun.*

Following Campbell's death in 1941, Raymond Bachman was appointed editor and publisher by Campbell's widow, Ann Boyd Campbell. A few years later Campbell's eldest son, Don, joined the staff as general manager. Soon thereafter his younger son, Jack, became executive editor. The Campbell brothers succeeded Bach-

man and acted as co-publishers until Jack's death in 1978.

The Columbian continues to be operated as a family-owned, independent newspaper with Don Campbell as publisher. A third generation of the Campbell family is active in the company, and Don's son, Scott, will succeed his father upon Don's retirement.

Herbert Campbell discontinued job printing in 1926 so that the firm could concentrate all of its efforts on publishing the newspaper. But when *The Columbian* became one of the first newspapers in the West to adopt the new offset printing method in 1968, commercial printing again became a viable endeavor.

In 1978 *The Columbian* purchased and remodeled a building adjacent to its operation. It later built an annex to that structure to house additional commercial presses.

Through technological innovation and dedicaton to providing a complete news source for the citizens of Clark County, *The Columbian* remains the only daily newspaper published in Vancouver. The Campbells intend to keep *The Columbian* a family-owned, independent newspaper—one of the few remaining in the Northwest.

KVAN AM 1550

Vancouver's contemporary adult music radio station, KVAN, provides Clark County residents with all kinds of information of local interest that they cannot find in any other media. Whether it is up-to-the-minute local news reporting or a day at the Clark County Fair, KVAN is there—and on the dial at AM 1550.

KVAN is the exclusive broadcast media in the metro market to tailor its news, weather, and sports to the residents of southwest Washington.

In 1963 the Federal Communications Commission granted a young but experienced radio man, Gordon Rogers, a license for KGAR Radio in Vancouver. His main goal was to develop a station for the Portland market.

An old house at 2808 Walnut in the Fruit Valley area became the studio, and Rogers began his all-news format broadcasts on Vancouver's new station, KGAR (K Gordon A. Rogers). In 1965 the station switched to top 40, which, at that time, with the popularity of the Beatles, was rock.

In its early years a major feature was the rebroadcasting of Fort Vancouver High School football games. Since the station could only be on the air during the day, the games were delayed until the following day. Tony Bacon was the color commentator for the games, and he also wrote local news copy for Rogers and hosted a weekly talk show.

In the mid-1970s Rogers wanted a full-time license. He was also looking to increase the station's power to 10,000 watts. He was aided in his discussions with the FCC by his attorneys, Jack Wynne and Bob Schaefer, who helped finance the expansion in return for half-interest in the business. The license application was awarded to KGAR in December 1976. The first day that the station was to broadcast with its 10,000 watts of power, the transmit-

The KVAN staff in June 1986 (left to right): Rick Lewis, account executive; Paul Duckworth, production manager; Warren Franklin, operations manager; Jeri Hovland, office manager; Don Walker, traffic; Ron Hughes, general manager; Dave Lee, public service director; Francine Pontious, account executive; Terry Finley, account executive; Rick Castle, account executive; and Kay Byers, account executive.

ter blew up and the station was off the air for the entire day.

On December 1, 1978, Capps Broadcasting acquired the station's license, and Gary Capps remains its owner today. Capps' vision for the station was to focus on the Clark County area and feature local news, public service announcements, and community involvement in the area.

In 1977 KVAN dropped its rock

Bill Cole (left) and Jeff Williams displaying the KVAN sign at the Clark County Fairgrounds.

music format and went to a modern country format, which lasted until April 1986 when a contemporary adult music format was adopted.

Since coming to Clark County, KVAN AM 1550 developed the Clark County Home Show in the spring of 1979, a tradition that has grown and been carried on ever since. That year also brought an expanded role at the Clark County

Fair, involvement and coverage of community parades and celebrations, and development of a larger Clark County news image. At the same time the station moved from its Walnut Street home to Orchards.

In June 1981 KGAR changed its call letters to KVAN. The new call letters reflect the philosophy of the station owner and management, and clearly identify the purpose of the station to be a Clark County station.

KVAN was the first Portland-Vancouver-area radio station to send an airplane aloft when Mount St. Helens erupted in May 1980. It also serves as the emergency broadcasting station for Clark County. The Seattle Seahawks broadcast all of their football games on KVAN. The station also carries Seattle Mariner baseball, University of Washington football games, and various local high school football and basketball contests.

KVAN AM 1550 is Clark County proud!

FRITO-LAY, INC.

In San Antonio, Texas, in September 1932 a quiet, imaginative man named Elmer Doolin discovered a corn chip made from basic corn dough (masa), which has been used as a bread for centuries by the Mexicans. Intuitively sensing the product would have broad consumer appeal, Doolin purchased the recipe for the Fritos-brand corn chips, along with 19 retail accounts, and the manufacturing equipment for $100. He set up his first Fritos plant in his mother's kitchen and produced about 10 pounds of corn chips an hour. Sales totaled some $8 to $10 per day, earning profits of about $2.

Coincidentally, young Herman Lay had started a potato chip business in Nashville the same year that Doolin began his enterprise. Lay used his 1928 automobile as a delivery truck to distribute potato chips he purchased wholesale from an Atlanta firm. His distributorship, which included northern Tennessee and southern Kentucky, survived the Depression and grew in its aftermath. First there were more routes, then more products. In 1936 Lay began to sell his own brand-name popcorn, and by the following year the Lay distributorship was a healthy, thriving business with 15 salesmen.

H.W. Lay & Company continued to prosper, added products, expanded, moved its headquarters to Atlanta, and introduced a completely new technique for potato chip manufacture—the continuous production line.

In 1945 the Frito Company awarded H.W. Lay & Company an exclusive franchise to manufacture and distribute Fritos brand corn chips in the Southeast, which was the beginning of a close affiliation that eventually led to a union of the two organizations. These successful snack food operations merged to become Frito-Lay, Inc., in 1961, and a period of burgeoning growth began. Sales soared, more plants were opened, new products multiplied, and more jobs were created.

Another major step was taken in July 1965, when Frito-Lay merged with the Pepsi-Cola Company, a leader in a closely related field. Together they became PepsiCo, Inc. Today both organizations operate as separate divisions of the worldwide parent corporation that does business in more than 125 nations.

Frito-Lay, Inc., opened its Vancouver facility in August 1972. Initially, 120 employees produced Lay's and Ruffles brand potato chips, Doritos brand tortilla chips, Fritos brand corn chips, and Cheetos brand fried cheese puffs. From an initial production volume of 15 million pounds per year, the Vancouver facility has grown to become one of the largest plants in the Frito-Lay system, employing more than 400 people and producing more than 50 million pounds of products each year.

The Vancouver operation is a dynamic part of the Frito-Lay division of PepsiCo. The firm has increased its sales from $500 million in 1974 to $8.1 billion in 1985.

Herman Lay, who died in December 1982, was not only a strong believer in the free enterprise system, he was also a prime example of how hard work and persistence made it work. The founder of the enterprise that bears his name often remarked that, "Business doesn't move, it flies." He would be proud of Frito-Lay's continued soaring growth and the important role it has played in communities such as Vancouver and throughout the country.

The Vancouver branch of Frito-Lay serves Idaho, Washington, Oregon, Northern California, Utah, Montana, Wyoming, and Alaska. Here a company tractor/trailer passes through the beautiful Columbia Gorge area.

The current Frito-Lay, Inc., plant in Vancouver after its 1984 expansion.

Frito-Lay Inc.   Vancouver, Washington

RED LION INNS

When co-founder Tod E. McClaskey opened the Thunderbird Coliseum Motor Inn in Portland in 1959, few observers gave the venture much chance for success. At the time the facility's location was relatively isolated and the founders were new to hotel management. Yet, utilizing a combination of strategies based on a firm commitment to quality, the founders beat the odds: Today that one motel has evolved into the renowned chain of Red Lion Inns—with 52 hotel-restaurant facilities throughout the West.

Despite the pessimistic predictions, the Portland Thunderbird was popular almost from the start. In fact, the original 89-room property has been expanded twice since its opening, now has 215 rooms, and has been renamed the Red Lion Inn

The inn's success prompted McClaskey to build several more Thunderbirds and Red Lion Inns in the Pacific Northwest in the 1960s and 1970s. One of them, the Red Lion at Sea-Tac Airport, opened its doors in 1969 as the largest of the company's hotels with 248 rooms; today it is still the largest with 850 rooms.

Soon after the Sea-Tac debut, the second Portland Thunderbird (now known as the Red Lion/Columbia River) was built on Hayden Island. It also was an immediate success and has since tripled in size. And when the Red Lion at Jantzen Beach began operations in 1978, the three Portland hotels formed one of the largest West Coast meeting/convention sites north of San Francisco. The expansion continued through the Pacific Northwest and down into the Sunbelt.

In 1985 major renovations at eight Red Lion properties were completed. One of these, Red Lion's La Posada Resort Hotel in Scottsdale, Arizona, now features a half-acre lagoon pool—one of the world's largest.

Red Lion Inns has always been headquartered in Vancouver. The firm's first offices were located in the Ford Building on Main Street. By the early 1970s the growth of the organization necessitated larger offices, and the headquarters was moved to 1115 Esther, current home of the Young Woman's Christian Association. Finally, in 1976, Red Lion moved to its present new building at 4001 Main Street.

In the highly competitive hotel/restaurant business, the company attributes its growth to strong, centralized management, careful planning, unwavering attention to detail, and the development of a superbly trained and enthusiastic work force.

From its corporate headquarters in Vancouver, Red Lion controls all operations that affect the quality of its separate inns. For example, the corporate commissary in Vancouver assures quality control of the meats, seafood, breads, and pastries served at Red Lion restaurants—the "hub" of most Red Lion Inns. Fresh midwestern beef is delivered by company trucks to Vancouver to be aged an

Tod E. McClaskey, co-founder and chairman of the board of the Red Lion Inns, beside loaves of French bread that have just come from the Olympic Deck oven. The special oven produces the thin-crust French bread served at all Red Lion Inns.

additional three to five weeks before it is custom-cut by Red Lion employees to the organization's exacting standards. About 400,000 pounds of beef per month, worth $1.5 million, go through the Vancouver plant.

A French pastry chef presides over the commissary's pastry kitchen, which serves all Vancouver-area Red Lions, including the Inn at the Quay, acquired in the early 1970s. He also supervises the baking of the French bread that has become one of Red Lion's hallmark menu items. In 1984 McCaskey sampled some excellent bread during a trip to Texas. As a result, an Olympic Deck oven, costing more than $100,000 and the only one of its kind on the West Coast, was installed in the Vancouver bakery. The oven combines the most advanced technology, built-in energy-saving devices, and traditional Old

World steam-heat baking that produces the thin crust characteristic of true French bread. Baked goods are shipped to facilities in the Portland-Vancouver area twice daily, while more distant Red Lions receive 80-percent-cooked loaves weekly; the baking process is then completed at the destination restaurant.

All of this attention to food quality produces results: Red Lions' food and beverage revenues account for about 50 percent of the company's total income, 15 to 20 percent higher than the industrywide figure.

The Vancouver headquarters branch and the graphics department in the Columbia Industrial Park design and produce the interiors for all Red Lion Inns. Oak and brass trimmings, etched and stained glass, metal sculptures, and intricate wood carv-

On June 15, 1959, the Thunderbird Motor Inn opened near the Coliseum in Portland, Oregon, setting off a series of successes, which are now legendary in the lodging industry.

ings adorn the Red Lion properties and help to create the chain's distinctive motif. Unlike many other hotel chains, Red Lion Inns are each decorated differently within the same overall theme, and each piece of art is an original.

Red Lion's personnel policies are another important factor in its success. With its general "promote from within" policy, the company has been able to motivate its 11,000 employees to provide the kind of high-quality service so crucial to satisfied guests and repeat business.

Today Red Lion has more than

11,000 guest rooms at 52 locations throughout the West, serving more than 350,000 lodgers every month. The company's purchase in 1985 by the investment banking firm of Kohlberg, Kravis Roberts & Company, McCaskey, and other investors (including pension funds of Oregon and Washington) will facilitate future plans for additional hotels in the West and gradual, steady growth across the rest of the nation.

Unlike 30 years ago, predictions for Red Lion's future can no longer be pessimistic: With a national reputation for excellence Red Lion Inns should continue to prosper. The company's expertise in hotel/restaurant management, design, and employee development should generate growth and profitability for years to come.

Patrons

The following individuals, companies, and organizations have made a valuable commitment to the quality of this publication. Windsor Publications and the Greater Vancouver Chamber of Commerce gratefully acknowledge their participation in *Vancouver on the Columbia: An Illustrated History.*

ADV Agency, Incorporated
Aluminum Company of America
  Vancouver Operations*
The Al Angelo Company*
Ed Austin National Can Corp.
Automotive Services, Inc.*
Blair, Schaefer, Hutchinson, Wynne,
  Potter & Horton*
Brown Seed Company
Diana Buell
Cadet Mfg. Co.
Cascade Distributing Co., Inc.
Christensen Motor Yacht Corp.
Clark County Genealogical Society
Clark Public Utility District*
Columbia Health Service*
Columbia Industrial Park*
Columbia Machine, Inc.*
The Columbian*
Robert Coy Properties
The Curlery Beauty Products
Dole Family Association
EOS
Vinton and Helen Erickson
Evergreen School District #114
Fazio Bros.
First Independent Bank
Fort Vancouver Chapter 19
  The Daughters of the Pioneers of
  Washington
Fort Vancouver Regional Library
Mrs. Homer P. Foster
Frito-Lay, Inc.*
Great Western Malting Co.*
Health Systems Group*

Hewlett Packard Company*
Hidden Brick Company*
Hillhaven Convalescent Center
Hospice of Clark County
International Systems, Inc.
Casey Jones Co., Inc.
Harold & Kay Kern
KVAN AM 1550*
Landerholm, Memovich, Lansverk
  and Whitesides, Inc., P.C.*
John A. Luetjen
Jim and Kay McClaskey
Mr. & Mrs. Wm. A. Maitland
R. James Mockford
Mulligan & Associates Appraisal Co.,
  Inc.
Nordstrom Vancouver Mall
North Tours
The Orthopaedic And Fracture
  Clinic
Pacific Telecom, Inc.*
Palena Associates, Inc.*
Vernon F. Peterson & Associates,
  P.S.*
Port of Vancouver*
Powell Distributing Co., Inc.

Red Lion Inns*
Ron's Century House
Paul Schurman Machine
SEH America, Inc.*
Smithrock Quarry, Inc.
Ken Storey, CPA
The Vancouver Clinic*
Vancouver Federal Savings Bank*
Vancouver Furniture*
Vancouver Mall*
Vancouver Mall Merchants
  Association
Vancouver Nissan*
Vancouver Realty, Inc.
Vancouver Seafood Inc.
Vancouver Woman's Club
Western Washington Agency
  Standard Insurance Company
Wolfe, Mullins, Hannan & Mercer,
  Inc., P.S., Attorneys at Law

*Partners in Progress of *Vancouver on the Columbia: An Illustrated History.* The histories of these companies and organizations appear in Chapter VII, beginning on page 109.

Appendix

Population Statistics

	Vancouver	Clark County
1860		2,384
1870		3,081
1880	1,722	5,490
1890	3,545	11,709
1900	3,126	13,419
1910	9,300	26,115
1920	12,627	32,805
1930	15,766	40,316
1940	18,788	49,852
1950	41,664	85,307
1960	32,464	93,809
1970	41,859	128,454
1980	42,834	192,227

The U.S. Census Bureau estimated the population of Clark County to be 94,898 in November 1943 and 98,923 in mid-May 1944, but some local sources figured the wartime population at considerably more than 100,000.

Vancouver's decline from 1950 to 1960 resulted from removal of wartime housing. McLoughlin Heights, the main shipyard workers' project, had been annexed January 1, 1950.

Additional Readings

I. BOOKS AND MANUSCRIPTS

Alley, B.F., and J.P. Munro-Fraser. *Clarke County, Washington Territory, 1885.* Reprint. Camas: Post Publishing Co., 1983.

Allworth, Louise, assisted by Bonnie Walden. *Battle Ground . . . In and Around.* Sponsored by the Federated Woman's Club of Battle Ground and the former Silver Star Junior Woman's Club. Dallas, Texas: Taylor Publishing Co., 1976.

Anderson, Marc. *Vancouver, A Pictorial History.* Norfolk, Virginia: Donning, 1983.

Barker, Burt Brown. *The McLoughlin Empire and Its Rulers.* Glendale, California: The Arthur H. Clark Co., 1959.

Binns, Archie. *Peter Skene Ogden, Fur Trader.* Portland, Oregon: Binford & Mort, 1967.

Bona, Milt. *Housing in War and Peace. The Story of Public Housing in Vancouver, Washington.* Vancouver: Housing Authority, City of Vancouver, 1972.

_____. *The Post Bicentennial (Camas-Washougal history).* Camas: Post Publications, 1976.

Burnham, H.J. *Early Land Titles in Vancouver, Washington.* Reprinted through courtesy of the Oregon Historical Society. Vancouver: Clark County Abstract & Title Co., 1947.

Claim of the Missionary Station of St. James, at Vancouver, Washington Territory, to 640 Acres of Land, Statement of Facts. n.p., n.d.

Clark County Historical Museum. "Trails and Early Roads and Other Stories." (by Z.F. Sakrison).

Clarke County Commissioners. *Clarke County in the Great State of Washington.* Portland, Oregon: The Holly Press, n.d.

Clarke County, Washington, The Italy of America. Vancouver: Columbian Publishing Co., Hitchcock Bros. Publishers, 1891.

Cline, Gloria Griffen. *Peter Skene Ogden and the Hudson's Bay Company.* Norman, Oklahoma: University of Oklahoma Press, 1974.

Douglas, Helen Holly. "A Survey of Some Steps in the Historical Development of the Vancouver, Wash., Schools." Unpublished dissertation. University of Washington, 1931.

Fogdall, Alberta Brooks. *Royal Family of the Columbia, Dr. John McLoughlin and His Family.* 1978. 2nd ed., Portland, Oregon: Binford & Mort, 1982.

Grafton, Richard N. *Vancouver-Built Ships of World War II.* Vol. 1, Escort Carriers (CVE); Vol. 2, Tank Landing Ships (LSTs). Compilation of various materials, some published, in Clark County Historical Museum.

Greater Vancouver Chamber of Commerce. *The Best of Both Worlds.* Woodland Hills, California: Windsor Publications, 1983.

Hazel Dell Community Study. "Growing Pains, The History of Hazel Dell." Mimeographed report, May 16, 1952.

Hidden, Robert Arthur and Margaret Ada. "A Hidden Memorial, Descendants of Andrew Hidden, of Rowley, Mass.: A Tribute to the Memory of Our Grandfather, Lowell Mason Hidden." Mimeographed. Vancouver: 1953.

Historical Committee, Glenwood-Laurin PTA. *Seven Bells Did Ring: A History of Barberton, Brush Prairie, Manor Union, Good Hope, Pleasant Valley and Glenwood School Districts.* Vancouver: Marque Printing Co., 1971.

History of the Spruce Production Division, United States Army. Introduction by Brigadier General Brice P. Disque. n.p., n.d.

Holman, Frederick V. *Dr. John McLoughlin, The Father of Oregon.* Cleveland, Ohio: The Arthur H. Clark Co., 1907.

Hussey, John A. *The History of Fort Vancouver and Its Physical Structure.* Tacoma: Washington State Historical Society, n.d.

_____. "The Hudson's Bay Company and The Pacific Northwest Indians." Fort Vancouver National Historic Site.

Jessett, Thomas E. *Reports and Letters of Herbert Beaver, 1836-38, Chaplain to the Hudson's Bay Company and Missionary to the Indians at Fort Vancouver.* Portland, Oregon: Champoeg Press, Reed College, 1959.

Jones, Roy F. *Wappato Indians of the Lower Columbia River Valley.* n.p., 1972.

Journal Kept by David Douglas During His Travels in North America, 1823-27. New York: Antiquarian Press, 1959.

Krenelka, Carol Ann. "Entertainments at Jantzen Beach Amusement Park, 1928-1970." Unpublished thesis. University of Oregon, 1981.

Landerholm, Carl. *Cayuse to Cadillac: Clark County History Told by Contemporaries.* 5 vols, 1947-1955. Manuscript, Fort Vancouver Regional Library, Vancouver.

_____. *Vancouver Area Chronology.* Vancouver: n.p., 1960.

McCrosson, Sister Mary of the Blessed Sacrament. *The Bell and the River.* Palo Alto, California: Pacific Books, 1957.

McLellan, Sister Mary de Sales. "Vancouver, Washington, 1846-70." Unpublished thesis. University of Oregon, 1935.

Marshall, John R., and Project Committee Authors. *A History of the Vancouver Public Schools.* Edited by Charles E. Scharff and Harold E.

Millen. Dallas, Texas: Taylor Publishing Co., 1975.

Matrix Engineers and Regional Planning Council of Clark County. "Environmental Impact Statement for a Planned Community in Cascade Park." Sponsored by Genstar Development, Inc., and the Hewlett-Packard Co. Vancouver: n.p., January 9, 1979.

Merk, Frederick, ed. *Fur Trade and Empire: George Simpson's Journal, 1824-25.* Revised ed. Cambridge, Massachusetts: The Belknap Press of Harvard University, 1968.

Miller, James D. "Some Factors Affecting the Growth of Vancouver, Washington." Unpublished thesis. Washington State College, 1936.

Parsons, Mark E. *Across Rushing Waters, A History of the Washougal River and Cape Horn.* Camas: Post-Record, 1982.

_____. *Looking Back: 100 Years of Camas and Washougal History.* Camas: Post Publications, 1983.

Person, Dorothy E. *From a Forest Clearing: A History of Hockinson School, and Tales of Yesteryear.* Vancouver: Marque Printing Co., 1971.

Ranck, Glenn N. *Legends and Traditions of Northwest History.* Vancouver: American Printing and Stationery Co., circa 1914.

Regional Planning Council of Clark County and U.S. Department of Housing and Urban Development, Portland Area Office. "Draft Environmental Impact Statement for Planned Community in Cascade Park." July 6, 1979.

Rich, E.E., ed. *The Champlain Society, Hudson's Bay Company Series. McLoughlin's Fort Vancouver Letters.* lst series, 1825-38; 2nd series, 1839-44; 3rd series, 1844-46. Toronto: The Champlain Society, 1941, 1943, 1944.

Roulstone, Thomas. "A Social History of Fort Vancouver." Unpublished thesis. Utah State University, Logan, Utah, 1975.

Schenk, John Frederick. "The Hudson's Bay Company in Oregon, 1821-60." Unpublished thesis. University of Oregon, 1932.

Shangle, Robert D. and Marian Berger. *Beautiful Vancouver U.S.A.* Beaverton, Oregon: Beautiful America Publishing Co., 1979.

U.S. Department of Interior, National Park Service, Denver Service Center. *Historic Furnishings Study, Armament and Furnishings of the Fort Vancouver Bastion.* By John A. Hussey. August 1973.

U.S. Department of Interior, National Park Service, Division of Publications. *Fort Vancouver.* By Archie Satterfield and David Lavender. Washington, D.C., 1981.

Van Arsdol, Ted. "Land of Prunes: The Rise and Fall of the Prune Industry in Clark County, Washington." Unpublished manuscript. Vancouver, 1973.

Vancouver City Planning Commission. *Vancouver, Columbia River's Port City for Homes and Industries.* Vancouver: Planning Commission, 1944.

Warner, Mikell De Lores Wormell, trans. Annotated by Harriet Duncan Munnick. *Catholic Church Records of the Pacific Northwest: Vancouver, Vols. I and II, and Stellamaris Mission.* St. Paul, Oregon: French Prairie Press, 1972.

Washington, D.C. National Archives. Record Group 98. Chaplain Franz J. Feinler. "Military History and Description of Vancouver Barracks, Wash." 1910-1911.

Welsh, William D. *A Brief History of Camas.* n.p., 1941.

Woodland Community Development Study. "Fields of Flowers and Forests of Firs." Woodland, May 13, 1958.

II. PERIODICALS

Bosn's Whistle. Kaiser shipyard, Vancouver, 1942-46. During part of this time the publication was in newspaper form.

Clark County History. Annual publication of Fort Vancouver Historical Society, 1960 to present. Printed at Camas and Vancouver.

The Coast, April 1909. This edition features the Vancouver area.

III. NEWSPAPERS

Clark County Sun. Files for scattered years of 1930s and 1940s at Clark County Historical Museum.

Pacific Weekly Censor, 1881.

Register, 1866-69, 1881-1902. The weekly was known as the *Clarke County Register* during some of this time and was the *Register-Democrat* in 1899-1901.

The Skirmisher. Published by Fourth Engineers Regiment, Vancouver Barracks, 1917.

Vancouver Columbian, 1890 to present.

Vancouver Independent, 1876-1910.

The material above is a selective and, in some instances, arbitrary listing of sources of Vancouver and Clark County history.

Many other published and unpublished items are available. Archaeological reports on excavations at Fort Vancouver Historic Site and the publications of the Clark County Geneaological Society are among items not included above. Fort Vancouver alone could require an extensive bibliography. The fur trading post is mentioned in many books by early-day travelers and in diaries of travelers to the Oregon country.

Index

Smith, Jedediah, 18
Smith Tower, 71
Sohns, Louis, 46, 65, 66, *66*
Sohon, Gustavus, 27
Sork, Elizabeth, 106
Spalding, Henry Harmon and Eliza
    Hart, 22, *23*
Spanish-American War, 76
Spokane, Portland and Seattle
    Railway, 8, 41, 51, 59
Sports, 56, 58
Spruce Production Division (U.S.
    Army), 52, 79, 80, *80*
Standard Theater, 56, 102
Standifer, Guy M., 78
Standifer Shipyard, 9, 52, 78, 79-80,
    79, 81
Stanislaus, Sister, 38, 39
Stanley, A.N., 103
Stanley, John Mix, 24
Star Brewery, 9
Star Stations, 43
Stout, George, *53*
Straub, Robert, 107
Strike, city and county workers', 10
Struve, H.G., 40
Student enrollment figures, 36
Sully, Alfred, 65
Sun (newspaper), 41-42
Swan Island Shipyard, 83

Task Force Systems, Inc., 54
Tektronix, Inc., 54, 106
Telegraph (newspaper), 40
Television stations, 43
Temperance movement, 33, *33*, 40
Ten Nights in a Barroom, 33
Thayer, C.S., *53*
Theaters, 56, *56*, 59, 60, 102-103,
    105, 106
Thunderbird motels, 72
Thursby, F.P., 16
Timberline Lodge, 82
Todd, John, 39
Tolmie, William Fraser, 22, 25
Tornado, 97
Toth, Peter, 96
Townsend, E.D., 31
Townsend, John K., 22
Tracy, Harry, 73
Treaty of 1855, 27
Tri-Met, 10
Trinity Episcopal Church, 30, 31
Troup, James, *68*
Truman, Harry (resort operator), 97

Umpqua River, 18
Unions, 54-55

United Church of Christ, 34, *90*
U.S.A. (theater), 60, 102
U.S. General Services
    Administration, 11
U.S. Geological Survey, 97
USS *Massachusetts,* 8

Valley Apartments, 80
Vancouver, George, 7, 16
Vancouver Avenue Baptist Church,
    35
Vancouver Barracks, 9, *9*, 11, 43, 65,
    79, 86, 102; mill, *80;* soldiers, *77*
Vancouver Civic Theatre, 60
Vancouver Fire Department, 55
Vancouver High School, *34,* 105
Vancouver Housing Authority, 9, 71,
    85, 86
Vancouver, Klickitat and Yakima
    Railroad, 8, 47, 65, 66
Vancouver Lake, 11, 17, 22
Vancouver Land Office, 9
Vancouver Mall, 104-105, 106
Vancouver Memorial Hospital, 10,
    105
Vancouver Port District, 8
Vancouver Sausage Festival, 60
Vancouver School District, 84
Vancouver-Sifton streetcar service,
    101
Vancouver Soda Works, *52*
Vanport, 9, 83, 86, *88,* 97; flood, *74,*
    75, 86, 97
Vollum, Howard, 73

Wakanasissi, 25
Wall, David, 45
Waremart food store, 97
Warre, Henry, 14
Washington and Oregon Company,
    49
Washington and Oregon Railroad
    (Northern Pacific), 8
Washington Growers Corporation,
    50-51
Washington Standard (newspaper),
    40
Washington State Department of
    Natural Resources, 78
Washington State Department of
    Social and Health Services, 10
Washington State Schools for the
    Deaf, 8, *36;* baseball team, *57*
Washington Territorial Legislature, 8
Washington Territory, 8
Washougal River Bridge, *87*
Waterfront, *100*
Weber, Warren, 90

Weinhard, Henry, 45
Western Electric Company, 53, 54
White, Elijah, 22
Whitman, Marcus and Narcissa, 22,
    23
Wilkes, Charles, 24-25
Williams, Harry, 72-73
Williams, Moses, 65
Williamson, Henry, 50
Windstorms, 10, 76, 97
Wineberg, John P., 52
Wineberg, William, 9, *73*
Wintler, Ella, 71-72, *71*
Wintler store, Michael, 45
Women's Christian Temperance
    Union, 33
Woodcutting, 45-46
Woodland, 81
Woolworth's, 105
Work, John, 19, 25
Works Progress Administration,
    81-82
World War I, 75, 78-80; Armistice
    Day, 80; flu epidemic, 75
World War II, 34, 36, 41, 42, 53, 54,
    60, 69, 75, 82, 83, 84-85, 106
Wright, Char, *97*
Wyeth, Nathaniel, 21

Yacolt Burn, 8, 77-78, *78*
Young brewery, Anton, *46*